A
CUBAN
STORY

A CUBAN STORY

MARCIA DEL MAR

JOHN F. BLAIR, Publisher
Winston-Salem, North Carolina

Library of Congress Catalog Card Number: 79-17551
ISBN 0-89587-011-8

Printed in the United States of America
by Heritage Printers, Inc.
Charlotte, North Carolina

Library of Congress Cataloging in Publication Data

Del Mar, Marcia, 1950–
    A Cuban story.

    1. Cuba–History–Revolution, 1959–Refugees.
2. Del Mar, Marcia, 1950–   3. Refugees–United
States–Biography. 4. Refugees–Cuba–Biography.
I. Title.
F1788.D43   325'.21'0924 [B]   79-17551
ISBN 0-89587-011-8

THIS BOOK IS DEDICATED
to the many casualties of revolution, and to those immigrants who have flocked to America in search of freedom.

and to Roseanne,

Marcia Del Mar
(818) 222 2100

Remember, remember always that all of us, and you and I especially, are descended from immigrants.

—Franklin Delano Roosevelt

1 I HAVE OFTEN ATTEMPTED to write about what we have gone through—a concise, personal manuscript that would bring together all the chaotic vignettes in my mind and give others an inkling of what the Cubans have experienced. How can one even begin, systematically and objectively, to put down on paper past events that have so little in common with present realities?

We are the forgotten immigrants—immigrants that don't hold vocal demonstrations, that don't make trouble; immigrants that don't publicly reveal our suffering and confusion. Yet we live our lives accompanied by the memories that haunt us, that we can't forget. We don't want to forget. We want to understand and be understood.

We have tended to congregate in southern cities—cities that, if only climatically, slightly resemble our native country. We remain, particularly our old people, in isolated enclaves, where we tend to repress or idealize our differentness for sheer survival. Cubans say with pride that in Miami one can live out one's whole existence without speaking a word of English. Those Cubans who do so preserve the last vestiges of an almost extinct culture, while detrimentally isolating themselves from the mainstream of contemporary American life.

Miami. To Americans, Miami evokes fantasies based on

travel brochures—tanned, buxom blondes luring dreamers to its shores, the smell of Coppertone and sweat permeating the air. Fun in the sun. How different a Miami we have known! But I must start my story at the very beginning.

I want to tell you about my people. Perhaps sharing what my family and friends have experienced will help you to understand and accept us better.

I look back with longing at Cuba, a country that will never be the same. We are a people altered irreversibly by events outside our control.

The tales that I will relate to you have all taken place. Certain names and places have been changed to shield those remaining in Cuba.

I write from a personal perspective, only about those whom I have known and loved—people like yourself, who are not public figures, people who lived their lives assuming themselves to be masters of their own destiny. Most were apolitical. Maybe that is where the blame, if any, lies. They viewed politics and government passively, as factors operating on a plane outside their immediate control. They accepted at first, with disinterest, changes that should have warned them of what was to come. Most were spectators rather than active participants in a power play that was to affect them directly and significantly. Most agree that events took place too quickly to assimilate. "We didn't know until it was too late," people tell me, hoping that this admission will excuse their inertia. Would any of them have acted differently had they been forewarned?

My elders vehemently agree that we should have stayed and fought to implement democracy in Cuba. "Everyone that escaped acted cowardly," they acknowledge to each other behind closed doors. We were merely unsophisticated. Communism was foreign and exotic to us, the common people. Our lack of familiarity with its ideology prevented

2

us from understanding the total picture. Once we fully understood its true meaning and implications, it was too late.

We, the members of Cuba's middle class, brought our misery upon ourselves. Blinded to the sorrow around us, uncaring and unconcerned, we insulated ourselves as a class. We shielded each other from the hunger and poverty of the peasants. Cuba was ripe for the revolution. The revolution came and we supported it, hoping that the inevitable changes would not impinge too much upon our comfort. The changes that followed left us dumbfounded, numb with disbelief. Disbelief led to fear and then to terror. Terror drove us away in hordes, making us think only of escape.

The socio-political climate of the island, prior to Fidel Castro, was dictated by corruption, nepotism, and violence. Historically, the Cuban attitude toward public office consisted of viewing the political arena as a source of personal profit. Electoral frauds were the norm. A series of charismatic but corrupt political leaders, coupled with the Cuban tendency to solve differences through violence, created a cycle of brutality and unrest. Civil discontent generated acts of terrorism. Government repression inevitably followed. Traditionally, those in power retaliated with measures ranging from the closing down of all schools to using torture and execution as an accepted means of coercion. These practices tended to culminate in coups, usually of a military nature, with the latest leader and his cabinet ruling the country through the wisdom of their whims.

The cycle perpetuated itself primarily because of a society characterized by self-interest, apathy, and disdain for political involvement. To be even peripherally involved in the political machinery carried an implication of immorality.

Prior to Fidel Castro's coming into power, Fulgencio Batista's elimination as head of the government was generally seen as the only solution to Cuba's problems. The people wished for a return of their civil rights as set forth in the Constitution of 1940. They longed for civil authority over civic matters, the withdrawal of troops from the schools, democratic elections, honesty within the ranks of public administrators, and a free press.

Proper housing, education, and health services for the poor, particularly for the *campesinos* or farmers, were scarce. The city poor worked long hours for low wages. The landless rural peasants depended primarily on sporadic employment. Government programs to help the destitute were virtually nonexistent. The poor were left at the mercy of the magnanimity of the rich. Unfortunately, charity efforts among the upper classes rarely resulted in significant change. The collective social consciousness historically present in America had never really been an integral component of Cuban society.

Fidel Castro embodied hope for the Cubans. His energy, youthfulness, and total dedication to the overthrow of Batista were, to Cubans, a source of inspiration and strength. Ignoring all risks, this handsome and brilliant young lawyer became a vehement spokesman against Batista's regime. He inspired the people by making poignant promises to bring democratic rule to Cuba. Fidel Castro began gradually to gain support among the people. He entrenched himself in the hills of Oriente, slowly building up a following. Guerrilla warfare in the rural areas and sabotage in the cities gathered momentum. Revolutionary activities during this period make up many of the memories of my childhood.

1957. It seemed as if every family in our neighborhood had already become disenchanted with the Batista regime. People wanted a change. We admired the American system of government and longed for a true leader to emerge. We wanted genuine democracy for our country. People longed

4

to walk confidently into a voting booth, assured of its inviolate sanctity. That voting in Cuba was a charade, a farce that had no meaning, saddened and frustrated my people.

Except for the heavily armed military forces, who solidly backed their leader, almost everyone that we knew personally despised Fulgencio Batista. People hated the lip service he paid to justice, the self-serving way he ruled the country. We abhorred him, this semi-illiterate army corporal whose cunning and ambition had propelled him to a position as the most powerful, and feared, man in Cuba.

For as long as I can remember, I could sense my parents' animosity towards Batista. They often ridiculed the numerous newspaper articles that praised his humanitarian efforts. They contemptuously spat on the ground whenever military parades passed triumphantly by our house.

We avidly followed American life through the many imported books and films available to us, and looked to America for guidance and inspiration. Two hundred years of peaceful governmental transitions left my parents in awe. Fiercely wishing the same for our country, they often marveled at America's ability to pull off such a miracle.

At family reunions, political debates dominated the conversation. Deep feelings of helplessness, however, overruled any serious plans for corrective measures. The tragic realization that our country's fate lay in the hands of the corrupt military was a never-ending source of agony for many. Even at that late date, though, some of the adults around me were able to rationalize away our circumstances. This rationalization was particularly easy for those whose lives prospered regardless of the political situation.

"Play deaf, dumb and blind . . . and survive," concluded the cynics.

"But we must do something," always replied my father.

Dad always took offense whenever someone espoused a

noninterfering attitude, while unwillingly acknowledging that it was indeed comforting to watch his own business prosper. His conscience was somewhat appeased by Mom's involvement in many philanthropic endeavors, from which she derived great personal satisfaction.

Aside from the political, life for us was good. Together we often took long swims at the paradisaical beaches that fringed the island. On Sundays we usually picnicked in Camaguey, at the foot of the Cantares Waterfall, whose source lay deep above the thick forests. We frequently rode horses in Pinar del Río, galloping beneath the hot, tropical sun through the lush fields of sugar cane and tobacco. During those times, cooled by the breezes that blew in from the Atlantic, we felt happy and momentarily free.

Food, at least for the middle class, was plentiful and reasonably priced. Thus, the three of us frequented weekly the numerous restaurants in the city which represented every imaginable cuisine.

Occasionally traveling abroad, we inevitably returned to our island-country convinced that it was the most beautiful spot on earth. To us, it was "The Pearl of the Antilles," as Columbus had once so aptly described our homeland.

My parents' dissatisfaction with the regime was kindled by the growing awareness that they were not alone in their discontent. There was great courage to be found in the realization that we were increasingly being surrounded by fearless spokesmen for freedom. Rumors began to circulate that the mountain rebels were daily gaining strength. The rebels, led by Fidel Castro, were gradually "liberating" the provinces adjoining Oriente. Traveling westward towards the capital, they marched on.

By the end of 1957, my parents' growing indignation, coupled with the successes being achieved in Oriente, prompted them to join the ever-swelling underground. The

6

time had come to jeopardize our own personal security for a grander vision, for a higher ideal. One sensed the growing optimism, and hope was infectious.

I recall the first time that I saw a photograph of "Fidelito," as Castro was fondly nicknamed. The reverence with which my mother handled his picture told me unequivocally that our savior had come forth.

At home, the long, balmy evenings began to be filled with anti-Batista activities. We spent the bulk of our free time packing arms, medicines, and food into large cartons. These were periodically picked up and delivered to Oriente by a friend of my father's, whose responsibility it was to make certain that the neighborhood's contributions reached the rebels.

We worked in semidarkness as a precaution against the military, who kept a constant watch for "revolutionaries." We labored diligently, children as well as adults, while listening to Castroite broadcasts from high above the hills of the Sierra Maestra. Those words of encouragement made us apply ourselves with zeal. "We cannot do it without you," said the messengers of freedom. We believed the faceless voices, applying ourselves harder than ever to our tasks.

The rebel successes in the eastern provinces prompted the government to intensify its search for Castro sympathizers. If you were even slightly suspected of being pro-Castro, you were subjected to frequent, unannounced house raids. You'd lie in bed at night wondering if your sleep would soon be interrupted by loud, sweating strangers who cradled their readied rifles in gleeful expectation.

Dad, feeling that it was no longer safe to continue helping the "box brigade," as the neighborhood kids fondly called our work, accepted no more assignments. But the raids nevertheless continued through the long summer nights.

I could often hear from inside my room soldiers' persistent

knocks at the door, intermingled with the cries of the cicadas.

Following my mother's instructions, I'd remain in my bed, pretending to be sound asleep. I often overheard Mami pleading with the soldiers in the hallway outside my door. Her assurance that only her sleeping daughter lay inside would merely provoke grunts of contempt. They'd usually opt for eagerly rushing into my room in search of a *revolucionario* or two, or perhaps an arsenal of ammunition ready for distribution.

One evening at dinner time, we heard an ear-piercing shot coming from our garden. Mami rose from her seat and grabbed me, spilling her glass of water on the tablecloth as she did so. Abruptly, she threw me onto the floor and lay heavily on top of me, holding her hand firmly over my mouth.

"Shh, shh," she kept repeating, trying to soothe me with the sound of her voice.

As the shot was fired, I had immediately turned to Dad to see his reaction. My first thoughts had been that maybe the bullet had found its way into the house through the open window which faced the garden. Fearing that he might be hit, I had looked to him for reassurance. He was fine; I wiggled around under Mami until I could see him moving about the room.

For the last two days, Dad had not been feeling well. He had developed a slight fever for which Mami kept treating him with herbs and alcohol rubs. Prior to dinner, she had been massaging him on the couch with the concoction. I could now smell its strong odor emanating from his body. He was wearing his blue-and-white-striped pajamas and the brown robe Aunt Alicia had recently bought him for his birthday.

Mami kept yelling for him to join us beneath the dining

room table. Tata, my nanny, who had been helping Mami serve the soup, was already crouching beneath the opposite side of the table. Tata's fat, dark face was flushed and she was sobbing loudly. I could hear her reciting the first two lines of Our Lord's Prayer, over and over again. I wondered if she had become so flustered as to forget the words, or if the sobbing itself was solely responsible for interrupting the flow of the prayer. The sound of her voice mingled with the gentle tune of the Lecuona album which continued to play on our phonograph, uninterrupted by the commotion outside.

Instead of joining us on the floor, Dad ran resolutely toward the front door. As no second shot had been heard, Mom unconvincingly speculated on the possibility that we had simply imagined it.

Although it was only minutes before Dad returned, to me it seemed as if he had been gone for hours. When he finally came back, he was holding an army rifle firmly in his hands. How incongruous it looked to have Dad fully armed, and wearing his cheerful cotton pajamas!

Suddenly we realized that Dad was being followed by a uniformed youth no older than fifteen. The shadowy beginnings of a mustache partially covered his upper lip. His face was ravaged by acne, the numerous red welts obviously aggravated by nervous picking. Sighing deeply while distractedly picking at his cheek, he walked meekly behind Dad.

The three of us slowly emerged from under the table, approaching Dad and the boy.

"We'll be having a guest for dinner. Tata, set a place for him," said Dad.

Tata exited toward the kitchen, making the sign of the cross and shaking her head in disbelief. Mom pulled out a chair for the boy and offered him a glass of milk, which he accepted with shaking hands.

Assigned by the government to keep a watch over our home, he had fallen asleep while on duty, and his rifle had accidentally gone off. Dad had found him, swearing and shaking in the darkness, trying to conceal himself behind the hibiscus bushes in the yard.

Juan, as the boy introduced himself, was originally from Matanzas Province and had recently come to the capital in search of a job. After praising Tata's now-cold soup, he told us about his struggles in the city, and how he had been encouraged by a friend to join the army. He did not know how to read or write, and had barely heard of Batista.

"He is a big shot general or something, no?" said Juan unconcerned, while hungrily devouring a slice of bread dipped in soup.

After dinner, he thanked us profusely, and laughingly begged us not to take his assignment too seriously.

"Look at it this way—I'll also be out there at night making sure you don't get robbed," he offered, smiling warmly as he spoke.

Juan and his rifle returned to his post behind the hibiscus for the remainder of the night. I spent the following evening playing checkers with him in the yard, keeping the mosquitoes and our unlikely guard company throughout the earlier part of his vigil.

Sometimes, civilian encounters with the military were fraught with danger. Unaware of the specifics, I nevertheless sensed my parents' fear and apprehension. As incidents always seemed to occur at night, I began to develop chronic insomnia. I would sit on my bed, staring at my bullet collection, daydreaming eleven-year-old dreams about the meaning of death and war. It was a sign of status among the children to have an extensive and varied bullet collection. The soldiers hurled them into the air during public parades.

We hoarded the bullets covetously, later trading them among ourselves for candy and toys.

I did not find it at all unusual as a child to have the military play an active role in our lives. Armed men were an integral part of the day. The tactics of Batista's regime simply followed the violent pattern which had characterized the island's political past.

My relationship with Isabel Mendoza illustrates how easily we children accepted the reality of the military, the possibility of violence. Isabel Mendoza was a young classmate of mine. We had grown up attending the same school and often played together in the afternoons when school let out. Isabel had long, thick braids and wore special orthopedic shoes. Her father was an influential member of Batista's inner circle so, understandably, he was always extremely concerned about the safety of his family. He rarely left the house, working out of the library and having his meals brought in by Andres, his fat and loyal bodyguard.

I could not then understand why the Mendozas never let Isabel come and play at my house.

Isabel was always picked up from school by a heavily armed motorcade. I remember Mr. Mendoza's dark and shiny limousine, flanked on each side by the ever-present, official-looking automobiles. The chauffeur never followed the same route back to the Mendozas'. Whenever I'd accompany Isabel home, we'd play at trying to outguess the route the driver planned to follow. We could never predict the way, as he often traveled for miles in one direction, only to backtrack and return by an entirely different route. Giggling in the spacious back seat, we'd tease the taciturn driver, who never once volunteered a word.

One day I asked Mami why the glass in the Mendozas' car windows seemed so thick and heavy to the touch.

"It's a special kind of glass, Marcia, in case revolucionarios take a shot at Isabel or her mother," Mami answered matter-of-factly.

Whenever we arrived at Isabel's, the tall iron gates at the entrance opened swiftly, almost as if by magic. I now guess that some kind of electronic device in the car was responsible for the gate's quick maneuvering. We would be ushered quickly inside the house, where a snack of milk and cookies usually awaited us.

A guard was always assigned to accompany us whenever we wanted to go and play in the yard. Mr. Mendoza had built a massive cement wall which enclosed the compound, making it almost impenetrable. Isabel and I sometimes asked to be allowed to play out on the street with the other neighborhood kids, but we were always forbidden to do so, so we obediently remained within the confines of the Mendozas' gilded cage.

We tended mostly to ignore the guards, concentrating instead on playing house with Isabel's numerous dolls—always, however, under constant scrutiny.

Isabel's two brothers enjoyed tremendously having the guards around. The boys played war games with their elaborate toy guns, and delighted in assigning the guards make-believe roles that complemented their games. One of their favorite pastimes was to pretend to be revolucionarios, whose goal it was to sneak successfully past the guards, into the kitchen, and eventually into the refrigerator. The military men usually humored the boys, standing rigidly on guard outside the back door, pretending not to notice the boys making their way toward the kitchen.

Whenever Mami came to get me for dinner, a thorough routine search was made of the car.

"A precautionary step against bombs," we had been told by one of the guards.

One of Isabel's biggest worries was what exactly would happen once she was allowed to date.

"Do you think the boys will mind if maybe just one guard tags along?" she asked me once, her round eyes wide and puzzled.

Mr. and Mrs. Mendoza were shot and killed right outside their front door the moment that Batista's government fell. I often worried about what had happened to Isabel, as she never returned to school. I wondered if her feet ever straightened out, or if she remained awkward and duckfooted forever.

For me, life in Havana before the revolution had been rigidly delineated even before my birth. It was presumed that I would attend a highly traditional Catholic high school, and that one year of language studies in either the United States or Switzerland would follow. Because I was merely a girl, college was not stressed. Cuban society made few allowances for a woman with intellectual pretensions. It was generally felt that too strong an interest in academic pursuits somehow detracted from one's femininity. Women almost took pride in their lack of factual knowledge concerning world affairs. Independence, ambition, aggressive impulses, and any propensity towards achievement and competition tended to be systematically curtailed through our rearing.

Girls were perennially instructed about the merits of the status quo. Our parents and teachers felt that the preservation of our femininity was a primary concern. Little girls rarely wore pants in Cuba. Instead, we were dressed in layers of constricting clothing that tended to limit our mobility and encumber our play. For a female to be allowed the freedom to explore her environment actively, as boys did, was almost a crime against nature. Now, listening to intimate conversations among elderly exiled women produces in me a reactive mixture of humor and rage. According to them, an intact hymen and a submissive personality still appear to be the crucial ingredients for achieving womanly success.

My father was a product of a traditional, old-country upbringing. His parents, originally from Asturia, a province in Spain, had fled to Cuba at the onset of the Spanish Civil War. As deeply religious pacifists, they had shunned active involvement in the war and had opted for immigration to the west. Charmed by the climate and the fertility of the soil, they had bought land in Camaguey. Their new hacienda dealt in cattle and in the processing of sugar cane.

The years brought prosperity to the household, with my father and his sisters growing up in an atmosphere of stability and wealth. At forty-two, my grandfather decided to return to Spain with his family for a short visit. They boarded an ocean liner bound for Spain. On the fourth day of the journey, my grandfather died of a sudden heart attack. Deciding not to bury him at sea, Grandmother chose to keep his body aboard in order that he might be interred in his native Spain. Immediately upon the ship's arrival, Grandfather was buried. On the following day, the family boarded another ship back to Cuba.

My grandmother's total ignorance regarding business matters led to the eventual bankruptcy of the hacienda. Dad, at the time only an adolescent, then took over responsibility for the family's fiscal affairs. He moved to the capital, where he worked at various odd jobs while attending the University of Havana. Perseverence and a knack for business led to his establishing Importaciones Internacionales, an importing firm. The business grew gradually into a lucrative venture, and my father's assets at the time of Castro's take-over were extensive but far from vast. My father took great pride in the kind of success he had achieved through honest, hard work. By American standards, we were part of the Cuban upper middle class.

My parents first met when Mother applied for a secretarial position at Importaciones Internacionales. She was of campesino origin, and her marriage to my father was viewed by many with a mixture of amazement and disdain. Mother, however, came to feel very much at home in Havana. I was born after three years of marriage. My parents were unable *only* to have any more children. *child*

Early memories of my mother are composed primarily of distinct sensory impressions: faint whiffs of talcum powder and intoxicating perfumes, the soft touch of fur, skirts that made crinkling paper noises, laughter and gaiety. She laughed easily in those days, a low, irrepressible, gurgling sort of laugh. My parents were happy, very much in love, and among family and friends. We were comfortable living the reality that they had built together for themselves, and for me.

Our home was adjacent to the ocean, on a rocky shoreline infested with sea urchins. The place was ideally suited for the periodic transporting of provisions to the hills. Once a week, always on Wednesday evenings, a small motorboat anchored near the shore and several men disembarked. They meticulously combed a specific area for packages wrapped in canvas which contained whatever had been collected during the previous week. My bedroom window overlooked the reef. I thoroughly enjoyed having school friends spend Wednesday nights with me. The predictability of those searching men, night scavengers crouching among ragged reefs, was far more enjoyable than reading or watching television. My guests always enjoyed the scenario. Hiding behind curtains, I displayed it to them proudly, often conveying the impression of having played an active role in its actual occurrence. One Wednesday night the men did not return. After a few days had elapsed, I casually asked my father about their whereabouts. The look of horror on his face told me more than his offhand comments about my having imagined their existence. I still wonder about the men's fates.

By the late fifties, guerrilla activity in Santiago had begun to permeate the adjoining provinces. The revolutionary fever was contagious. It was becoming impossible for the government to curb the enthusiasm being generated by the ever-increasing possibility that Fidel Castro might emerge victorious. Violent acts against the government grew more frequent. Anti-Batista sentiment among the people became almost universal. My family, like others, prayed daily to "la Caridad," our patron saint, to rid us of Fulgencio Batista.

On December 31, 1958, a sumptuous New Year's Eve party was held at the Palacio Real in Havana. All top government officials and their wives were asked to attend. The fighting had reached the outskirts of Havana, and those in attendance could vaguely hear the rumbling of ammunition in the distance. As the party drew to a close, Batista bid his evening farewells with equanimity. All those present were reassured as to the ongoing strength of his regime. That was the last evening Fulgencio Batista spent on the island. It had been prearranged that an airplane would fly him out of Cuba that very night. Batista died a few years later in Portugal, a rich man. His last days were spent in opulence, playing golf and sanctimoniously bemoaning the forceful take-over by Fidel Castro Ruz.

As always, we spent that particular New Year's Eve at my Aunt Alicia's. My parents' numerous brothers and sisters were there, accompanied by their many children. Uncle Miguel spent the whole day digging a pit in the back yard so that we could properly roast Cuba's traditional New Year's pig. Everyone sat out on the back porch, drinking rum and listening to my cousin Flavio play the guitar.

There was a full moon that night, so we could clearly see my younger cousins playing hide-and-seek among the tamarind trees. Choosing to remain in the company of the adults, I sat at Mami's feet and let her comb out my long, tangled hair as she talked. Through the open windows we could hear the sound of a crying baby coming from an upstairs bedroom.

"Little Rafael has the hiccups. Don't worry, I've already placed a wet thread on his forehead. It should be all right soon," volunteered Cousin Tina, as she lazily swung on the hammock. The older women nodded in agreement. It was reassuring to know that Tina knew just what to do to help little Rafael with his hiccups. Rafael was Tina's third son. The family was in agreement that Tina must be very *caliente*. It was said that only very passionate women bore sons.

It was always so cozy at Aunt Alicia's! Her hospitality knew no bounds. The house was usually full of relatives whose exact blood relation to each other was often a complete mystery. Sometimes there were as many as fifty people who, in theory, were "family" at Alicia's.

"This is Cousin Francisco, from Oriente, Aunt Carmen's youngest boy," went the introductions.

"This is your second cousin Marco, from Pinar del Río, Uncle Jesus' godchild, who is going to be staying here in the capital with us for a while," interjected one of my many aunts.

These extended family visits often lasted for months. Cousin Juanita, from somewhere in Santa Clara, had been staying at Aunt Alicia's for years. Not even Mami knew Juanita's exact relationship to the family, yet nobody seemed to care. As Juanita was reputed to make the best *boliche* in town, stuffing the slices of ham into the meat with the mastery of a chef, her precise genealogy was of little concern. At Aunt Alicia's, you always sensed the warmth with which family members related to one another and to the many new arrivals.

"This is your Cousin Rita, the *hija de crianza*, or daughter of rearing rather than of birth, of your Aunt Francisca."

Children of *crianza* were thought of as integral parts of the family. It did not matter how they came to be raised by a particular family member. They were incorporated quickly and without reservations. Usually, they were the children of friends or relatives long since dead. Often, they were the illegitimate offspring of actual blood relatives. At times they were the children of anonymous street beggars, whose thickly bundled little bodies were left at the family's doorstep with a simple note. The beggars knew that their children would be well cared for at Alicia's.

As usual, political debates went on through the night.

"Cousin Francisco just got back from Oriente, and he says that the whole province considers itself already 'liberated' from Batista," said Alicia, while Francisco gnawed on a chicken bone and nodded.

"Members of the military have voluntarily discarded their uniforms and joined the people," added Uncle Miguel with excitement.

"The pot is about to boil over. God help us when the fighting reaches Havana," cryptically predicted one of the cousins.

Before our dinner of roasted pig, Aunt Alicia asked us all to offer a minute of silent prayer for a peaceful transition from Batista to what was to come. Holding hands in a circle, we bowed our heads and prayed that the inevitable disposal of Batista take place in a smooth and orderly manner.

18

On the morning of January 1, 1959, news of Castro's victory was broadcast with glee. There was drinking and singing in the streets. The green-clad soldiers entered the city accompanied by cheering mobs. Women threw multicolored flowers into the happy crowd from wrought-iron balconies. Everyone felt miraculously saved from tyranny. Fidel Castro spoke in the public plaza. He sounded marvelously patriotic, humanitarian, and concerned. We listened to him speak in awe. During the speech, white love birds were released into the crowd. One of the birds flew towards him, gently perching on his right shoulder. The crowds went wild with joy. All of us there that day interpreted the scene as the most positive of omens. The men surrounding him wore rosary beads around their necks. The savior and his disciples had emerged victorious. They had arrived in the capital, enthralling their supporters with gimmickry and promises of democracy that were never to be fulfilled.

My parents were ecstatic once Batista's overthrow became a reality.

"Everything is going to be different now, Marcia," Papi assured me with confidence.

Our neighbors held "liberation parties," flying torn, mildewy flags insolently out their windows. For the celebrations, people baked cakes in the shape of the island, partitioning the provinces into segments overflowing with ice cream. Fireworks went off intermittently for weeks. Hardly anyone went to work. What better excuse for celebrating than Batista's elimination! Most shopkeepers closed their doors temporarily, and those who remained open for business advertised special sales in honor of the revolution.

"We're a free country!" strangers shouted at you from their cars, blowing their horns loudly as confirmation. Everyone was certain that free elections would soon be held.

19

People discussed potential candidates among themselves. There was no question in anyone's mind, however, that if Fidelito ran for office, he would be unanimously elected.

The months went by without the promised elections taking place. Castro soon named Dr. Carlos Dorticos as president of a provisional government. He was to head the government until the elections.

"Fidelito is just waiting for things to stabilize," people speculated.

"Elections will soon come," everyone agreed.

Changes began to take place, but not quite as anticipated. The country's transformation was so gradual, so subtle at first, that it was difficult for people to grasp fully its greater meaning.

"Fidelito says that the country is just not ready for elections," meekly said those who still wanted to believe we were at the dawn of a new era.

People continued to argue heatedly the merits of such and such a candidate, but the growing realization that elections might never come finally began to take hold.

"Fidelito wants to help the campesinos, so he is just passing certain laws prior to the elections. He wants to make sure they're implemented," said Uncle Miguel one night at our house, with little conviction.

Cousin Francisco was lethargically blowing smoke rings as he smoked a cigar. Uncle Miguel's words made his face contort into an unpleasant grimace.

"Wake up, Miguel, it's the same old shit," he answered, furiously stamping out his cigar.

Mami reminded the men that I was in the room, gently suggesting that they discuss something else besides politics.

Everyone ignored Mami and continued to argue, their voices growing louder and their words more bitter. Mami finally told me to leave the room, which I did, wishing that

_1960_

young Juan were still watching over our house so we could play checkers.

By the winter of 1960, nobody talked about the forthcoming elections anymore. People still wanted to believe in Fidelito, however, and besides, everyone agreed that helping the campesinos was a matter of top priority. So life, basically, went on as before, just slightly marred by an insidious and ever-growing disenchantment.

By the end of the year, forty percent of Cuba's land would be under government management. "For the benefit of the _campesinos_," we were told. Newspapers were taken over, and broadcasting was strictly controlled. As had been the case prior to Castro, it became once more a crime, punishable by law, to criticize the new regime. Energetic steps began to be taken to obliterate Cuba's bourgeoisie for "our own good."

People began trying to get out of the country in whatever way they could.

40% of Cuba's land gov't

2

FOR A WHILE AFTER THE revolution, I continued to attend the Mother of Jesus School in the Biltmore district of Havana. The nuns at my school were initially elated over Fidel Castro's victory. Abhorring Batista's regime and its atrocities, they had strongly supported Castro's revolution. We were given a week off from school in celebration of his victory. Then a Mass in his honor was held in the chapel. We said a special prayer on that day, thanking God for ridding us of Batista. The school became involved in organizing an extensive community campaign to amass badly needed agricultural equipment for the campesinos. Fidel Castro had pleaded with the people over the radio to share in helping the campesinos. The response at my school was overwhelming.

A ceremony was held in the school yard. All our parents, having donated expensive agricultural equipment for the occasion, were present. Each child stood solemnly in front of the gift his parents had contributed. We all felt we were an important part of the revolution, gathered there in front of the tractors and machinery while the National Anthem was played, off key, by the Mother of Jesus Band.

I was certain on that day that Fidel personally knew about our ceremony. How proud he must be of us, I thought, while waiting for my name to be called.

The Mother of Jesus nuns eventually came to regret their unconditional support of Fidel Castro. They were imprisoned two years later for three weeks in the school basement. Mattresses were brought in for them to sleep on. Their hair was shaved. Castro had outlawed the public religious processions that were traditionally held throughout the year, and the nuns had vehemently voiced their strong opposition. The government, feeling that they were instigating subversive activities against the regime, placed them under house arrest.

A few months after Castro's take-over, a new administration was appointed by the Department of Education to oversee the school. A curriculum was implemented which stressed political awareness. We began to use new educational materials geared toward that goal. Every story read, game played, or assignment given seemed designed to develop within us an almost fanatical sense of moral obligation toward the state. Activities we engaged in, however harmless, were interpreted to us by our teachers as either in accordance with the spirit of the revolution or counterrevolutionary. We were subtly drilled through group discussions on the merits of the changes daily taking place around us. We worked after class for two hours in the school's garden in order that we might learn firsthand the rigors of manual labor.

The values that had been stressed by the nuns before the revolution no longer seemed to matter. The new order was what was progressive and sound. The fact that the state was of greater importance than family, friendship, or religion was always emphasized. We had admired and respected the Americans for their democratic system of government and accomplishments. Now we were told by our teachers that they were directly responsible for most of our country's problems. The United States went from father figure to scapegoat. We wondered about America and its people. They were pictured to us as devils; I would have actually believed in those days that the Yankees ate their young. I shudder as I remember the blind hatred that caused a classmate of mine to draw a red demon in art class. Instead of holding a pitchfork, it carried an American flag. She was praised very highly by our instructor.

In retrospect, I wonder about the subtle differences between education and indoctrination. I would not describe as education my last few months of studies at the Mother of Jesus School. The daily recess hour was altered to include such military exercises as marching and the proficient manipulation of firearms. According to our teachers, these skills were now prerequisities of good citizenship. Our scholastic preparation had as its goal the development of total citizens. We were expected to perpetuate and expound Fidel Castro's doctrines. We were specifically asked to report to the school on the content of the adult conversations overheard in our homes. A system of gold and silver stars was begun which rewarded the children's thoroughness in this matter of informing on their parents. We were told how proud Papa Fidel was made to feel whenever he learned of our devotion. Furthermore, we were told that we were actually helping our parents whenever we reported any of their unhappiness with the government. "Adult teachers" would make certain that our families better understood the changes that were taking place. This re-education would make our parents happier and more content. Our teachers' explanation made a great deal of sense to all of us. What could be better than getting stars at school for helping our parents feel better?

I remember an incident concerning my favorite teacher at school. We all knew that Miss Elena had become heavily involved in the political scene. She had hung a large photograph of our country's new leader in the front of the classroom and daily brought in with her an assortment of tropical flowers hastily gathered on her way to school. She always placed the flowers in a glass vase before Fidel's picture. Children who followed her example were commended in front of the class. The praise and attention we received made us bloom even more effervescently than the flowers. To bring flowers for Fidel transformed us into good children in Miss Elena's eyes.

One day after lunch, Miss Elena told our class that we were now to play a most unusual game. I remember sensing the excitement that her cryptic statement produced. It would be a game that was both fun and educational, she elaborated. Miss Elena asked that all twelve of us sit on the floor encircling her.

"Close your eyes and concentrate really hard on asking God to bring you some candy," she said.

We did just as she requested for a few minutes. She then told us to open our eyes and look around for the candy. Our disappointment was great, as no sweets had materialized. Groans were heard coming from some of the children.

"Now close your eyes again. This time ask Papa Fidel for candy," she told us as she smiled.

I did as I was told for only a few seconds. Growing impatient, I half opened my eyes, squinting to avoid detection. I plainly saw Miss Elena go quietly around the circle, depositing a handful of chocolate kisses before each student. Her task completed, she inconspicuously returned to her original place.

"Now open your eyes, class," she said brightly.

The children were awed at what they saw. Squeals of delight could be heard as they greedily unwrapped their candy.

"Remember this day whenever you feel the urge to pray. Don't waste your time praying to someone who can't hear *pray to Papa Fidel*

you. Work hard for Papa Fidel and all your prayers will be answered," she told us. The bell for the next class rang and we were excused.

When I got home that afternoon and related the puzzling incident to Mami, all she did was hug me tightly and cry.

Later on in the year my mother received a frantic telephone call from Aunt Olga. My cousin Roberto had solemnly warned Aunt Olga about the growing complaints against the government he heard at home. Unless they were stopped, he warned his mother, he would feel it his duty to report her to his school. Roberto was an active member of *Los Pioneros*, a new children's militia organization. He took great pride in his absolute loyalty to the pioneros and in his adherence to their Code of Conduct. Roberto piteously begged Aunt Olga not to place him in the awkward position of having to choose between the Pioneros and home. He was twelve years old at the time.

After his take-over, Castro had almost immediately addressed himself to the systematic annihilation of those members of the opposition that still remained on the island. Hundreds of military and civic leaders, even those who had been only peripherally involved with Batista's government, were executed by firing squad on national television.

I vividly recall the executions of those men, never legally tried. The killings, carried out very efficiently, were orchestrated for all of us to see. The prisoners were brought blindfolded in groups of six. They were made to stand side by side against a wall and were then methodically shot. It was more than a purge. It was a statement of power and subjugation. The number of men killed was immense. The viewing audience became desensitized to the televised horror. People turned off their television sets from sheer monotony.

26

By the fall of 1961, it seemed as if all that mattered anymore was to prove one's loyalty to the government. Reporting individuals one considered counterrevolutionary became the most effective way to gain recognition and prestige. A personal grudge against a neighbor could be turned into something profitable. If you reported someone as being counterrevolutionary, not only was the person reported imprisoned, but you were certain to gain for yourself recognition and praise.

It became extremely prestigious to become a member of the Cuban Communist Party. Party membership proved beyond a doubt one's devotion to the government. It also assured for its members a number of privileges not otherwise available. Party members became the new Cuban elite. To gain membership a person had to be nominated by his fellow workers. No member could belong to any religious group. Having a relative who was a Party member in good standing was in itself an asset.

One of the advantages of Party membership became particularly evident when the rationing system went into effect in 1961. As basic necessities were by then in short supply, every family was issued a standardized rationing booklet. In it, all that one was allowed to buy was itemized and tabulated. People were no longer able to purchase clothing or food freely. In time, the term "rationing manual," which implied scarcity, was replaced by "provisions manual." The new label held a more positive connotation, but the purpose of the booklet remained the same.

Equality of opportunity was no longer enough. Equality of outcome was what mattered. With the island's decreased trade and new emphasis on total equalization, all purchases, whenever available, were dictated by the manual. Two days a month were set aside so that we could purchase rationed non-food items.

The following is a random sample from a provisions manual of products and their allotted amounts:

1 pair of shoes a year

1 ½ ounces of coffee a week

1 whole chicken a month

½ pound of bread a day

2 ½ pounds of fish a week

1 pack of cigarettes a week

1 dozen eggs a month

½ pound of meat a week

6 oranges a week

Refrigerators, television sets, and stereos were now labeled luxury items. If your co-workers vouched for your loyalty, your name was added to the Luxury Item waiting list.

The sick could obtain a medical dispensation which increased their ration for the week. They were also given a liter of milk every two days. Normally, only children and those over sixty received milk. Often, nothing was available for as long as five days. A shortage was usually followed by two or three days of plenitude. Bananas and beans always seemed to be available, so many families depended on them to get through any given week. Ironically, sugar, Cuba's most important export commodity, was usually strictly rationed. Clothing was almost impossible to obtain. Textile manufacturing had never really flourished in Cuba, so in the past we had depended on American imports to fulfill the island's needs.

When rumors circulated that a certain store had just received a shipment of shirts, hundreds of persons flocked there with their manuals and stood in line in front of the store. Often, the wait could take as long as three days. Members of any given family usually rotated waiting their turn. This rotation allowed everyone to return home for a few hours of sleep in between the waits. Vigils usually continued throughout the night, with long lines surrounding the stores in concentric circles. When supplies were exhausted, all those still waiting were curtly sent away. Lines formed and reformed, with demand always exceeding supply.

One day Grandfather and I patiently waited our turn in a line formed for the purpose of distributing bread. A young man, impatient and obviously hungry, attempted to slip into the front of the line ahead of an older woman. Flying into a tearful rage she took off her high-heeled shoes and began to beat him over the head with them. The heel of one shoe penetrated his skull, and the man slumped to the curb, unconscious. All who were waiting stood impassively by, watching the blood gradually stain the sidewalk red. People were fearful of losing their turn in a line that had already lasted two days; nobody dared approach the dying man. Several hours elapsed before the body was inconspicuously removed by the authorities.

We remained in line, unwilling spectators to a death without meaning. I remember how hot the day was. The blood that poured out of the man's skull soon mingled with his hair and began to dry. Flies swarmed about his head, wildly buzzing. They seemed, like us, to be eagerly waiting for something to eat. Feeling nauseous, I told Grandfather in a low voice that I wasn't very hungry anymore. Let's go home, I begged.

Grandfather clasped my hand tightly and told me that I must try to be strong.

"He got what he deserved, Marcia. You don't buck the system. Don't look at him anymore. The line is moving more swiftly now. We'll soon be going home."

To break the solemn mood, Grandfather began to hum a popular tune. Everyone in line soon followed his example. The crowd continued to sing in unison, accompanied by the melodious buzzing of the flies.

Lines in which the interested parties rotated a turn could last as long as a full week, with no guarantee that the wait would be worthwhile. Once my aunt and uncle needed to get a birthday toy for my young cousin Sylvia. After several days of rotating turns in line for such a "luxury item," their efforts were rewarded with a toy gun for Sylvia. The supply of dolls and other more appropriate playthings was exhausted. The store clerk assigned the gun to the despairing family saying, "Having your little girl play with this toy will make her better appreciate Fidel's efforts."

As supplies dwindled with time, operating grocery stores were divided between those open to the general public and those solely at the disposal of foreign visitors and party members. How utterly frustrating it was to drive past stores bulging with delicacies not even itemized in the manual! Transparent glass panes made it possible to savor from a distance everything from roasts to imported champagne and caviar.

An evening drive around Embassy Row inevitably revealed ill-clad individuals groping among the dignitaries' trash cans. They were like underfed alley cats pathetically scrounging for scraps of food. Prior to Fidel Castro, hunger and poverty had characterized life for many Cubans. After Castro's take-over, all but party members and government officials seemed to suffer from some degree of deprivation and want.

I grew to hate the ordeal of walking from our house to the place where I nightly took my ballet lessons. Mami, who usually accompanied me, began to fear our evening walks as well. The dancing school was located about three quarters of a mile from our house. It became nearly impossible to make the trip without being accosted by beggars.

"*Dame dinero o algo de comer, niña*," they said, tugging at my dress. They all seemed to want our help—help that we were unable to provide because of their sheer numbers. We must think first of ourselves, said every adult around me. I

soon learned that survival required you to numb your in-
stincts, to pretend that all was as it had been before. I often
remembered the advice given me: "Play deaf, dumb, and
blind . . . and survive."

It must be nearly impossible for those reared on a steady
diet of capitalism to imagine life in a society that has func-
tionally abolished the concept of private property. Let political scientists and demagogues discuss among themselves
the ideological differences between capitalism, Marxism, and
Castroism. It is not my purpose to discuss the pros and cons
of utopian ideas which might project idyllic visions of what
"The Good Life" is or could be. I write solely about the
mundane realities of enforcing one particular man's dream—
a dream that although possibly well-intentioned, nevertheless lost in its implementation a sense of proportion and
humanity. An elderly street vendor being forcefully taken
away by green-clad militiamen said it all very aptly: "I have
seen many governments come and go while I peddled my
wares and didn't bother anybody. Why the hell can't I
anymore?"

A friend of my family's was a grocer in Cuba. He had in-
herited his modest store from his father and in it sold primarily fruits, vegetables, and fish. When these products became
scarce, he would candidly inform prospective clients, *"No
hay"* ("There isn't any"). One afternoon he received an
unannounced visit from an underling of the Ministry of
Foods who "recommended" that he say instead, *"Se acabó"*
("I have run out").

The shortages created some interesting situations. Once
my grandfather was unsuspectingly riding a public bus in
downtown Havana along with twenty or more other passengers. Two armed men forcibly entered the bus and demanded that all those aboard remove their shoes. Puzzled,
the group complied. While one man pointed a gun threaten-

31

ingly at the bewildered passengers, the other methodically and carefully collected all the shoes and stuffed them into a large plastic bag. A passenger sarcastically commented on the unusual nature of the robbery, adding that it was just as well that he had spent all his money before boarding the bus. The mention of money made the men laugh.

"We can get a hundred pesos a pair for these shoes in the black market, even if they're worn. But better still, we can trade them directly for food," one of them said.

"What's the point of money itself when you can't buy what you need?" said the other.

Those just robbed agreed. The thieves departed with their loot, and the passengers returned their wallets and coin purses to their respective pockets, reconciling themselves to the loss of their shoes.

The people of Cuba have always prided themselves on their ability to transform the most tragic event into *Choteos Criollos*—that is, to be able to turn what disturbs them into comedy through jest. They usually achieve this transformation by making up amusing songs about whatever is upsetting them. When Castro appropriated all funeral homes, he declared that burials were to be conducted free of charge. The following choteo began to circulate among the people: "Fidel is the sort of ruler who kills his subjects by starvation, but who willingly buries them free."

Strict measures were taken to abolish all choteos, particularly those being sung by people assembled with their rationing manuals in lines outside stores. An ordinance was passed by the Committee for the Defense of the Revolution which encouraged those loyal to the state to strike any offender publicly on the lips. One day, while waiting his turn in a vegetable line, a young man began to chotear loudly about his predicament. Suddenly a woman, a member of the Defense Committee, approached him and struck him

32

harshly in the face with her purse. The young man's lip was cut and he began to bleed profusely. With his handkerchief, he attempted to stop the blood, which was by then soaking the front of his shirt. He seemed stunned and withdrew from the line, disappearing into the crowd. Minutes later he returned, extremely pale and subdued, and inquired as to the culprit's whereabouts. The woman, challenging him, stepped forward and said to him, "I hit you, so what?" No sooner had she finished the sentence than the youth produced a sharp knife which he had concealed in his shirt. He stabbed her repeatedly, while hysterically laughing and crying. He was finally detained by plain-clothes Committee members, and it was never learned whether he was imprisoned or killed. Incidents such as robberies, car accidents, and crimes of passion were no longer authorized newspaper subjects.

I begged my parents not to suggest anymore that I accompany Grandfather on his biweekly trips to the food line. One never knew what passions would flair, what incidents would disrupt the uneventfulness of the day. I grew more and more anxious and afraid.

My parents respected my wishes. Whenever I ate a slice of warm bread or a freshly picked banana, however, I inevitably speculated about the possible tragedy that must have accompanied its procurement.

Not all of Castro's reforms caused discontent; a number of changes improved the people's lot substantially. For instance, although one still paid for gas and electricity, water was distributed without charge. In addition to free burials, there were free marriage ceremonies, though the large number of ceremonies needing to be performed resulted in mass marriages becoming the rule rather than the exception. Women workers were given three months off with pay prior to delivering their babies, and three months of leave after

33

the children were born. By the time a child walked and fed himself, he could attend a government-run day-care center free of charge. All educational institutions and health-care facilities were free of charge. Doctors, however, could not enter into private practice. They now received free medical training from the government, and profit-making in the health-care system was viewed as abusive.

Theoretically, medicines were also free, but in reality most were extremely difficult to obtain, as imports were generally unavailable. My grandmother, a diabetic, died a gradual and painful death in 1962 due to the lack of proper medication. Dosages of insulin obtained through the black market were both minimal and unreliable. Friends already exiled in America attempted to send her medications through the mail. The packages were always confiscated prior to their arrival. Initially, Grandmother went blind; then it became very difficult for her to get about. As new symptoms surfaced, she became fully bedridden. She was in great pain up to the last minute. Grandfather did all he could; he fed her and bathed her daily. He would read books to her and lovingly comb her hair. When she died, he locked himself in his bedroom for three days. It took him about two months to be able to talk about her or to look at photographs of her without breaking down.

In 1961, however, future eventualities such as my grandmother's death were only vaguely imagined. People were busy coping with food shortages and with upheavals in the legal system. Certain people, such as those in the midst of getting a divorce, found themselves casualties of a social experiment that lacked precedents. A more common problem, one that affected nearly everyone in Cuba, was housing.

A series of laws were passed which drastically changed the concept of private property. If a person had rented his home prior to the revolution, he was given the opportunity

34

of continuing rental payments for five years. After that period he became the home's "owner." Owners, however, were not allowed to sell or rent their property for profit, although they could occupy it free of charge. If a person wanted to move, he could trade his home, with government authorization, for that of another willing "homeowner." For anyone choosing to maintain tenant status, a fixed rent consisting of ten percent of his monthly income was universally established. Understandably, these sudden and drastic changes resulted in absolute chaos. Such uncertain and nebulous circumstances led to problems of redefining the status of home ownership for a large portion of the population. As the new ordinance also affected home furnishings, personal belongings had to be itemized in every household, and up-to-date lists kept. New homes were assigned on the basis of work output and "attitude."

My maternal grandparents had years before built a small weekend cottage in Boca Ciega, a fishing village near Varadero Beach. Throughout the years, the little house had hosted innumerable family gatherings and had acquired immense emotional significance for us all. The new housing laws permitted the ownership of just one home per family, so the Boca Ciega cottage was quickly confiscated.

My grandparents' permanent home was located in the heart of the business district. It was an ancient structure, and its refrigerator was a malfunctioning relic which they had meant to dispose of since before the revolution. After the housing law came into existence, my grandfather requested permission to exchange the old refrigerator for the new one he had installed at the cottage. It took three days of bureaucratic red tape before government officials finally granted him permission. The cottage had been locked up by the authorities so nobody could get in. While transporting the unit from the cottage to town, we were twice stopped by

35

the authorities, who requested that we show them our permit. By that time it was evident to my family that conditions had deteriorated to a point where civil liberties no longer included the most basic of freedoms previously taken for granted. We continued the remaining drive home mostly in bewildered silence, with those of us in the car pondering the direction the new regime was taking.

The fondest of my memories of Cuba concerns my dollhouse. It was an exact replica of the main house. Meticulously furnished, it had pink and white checkered curtains, a fully equipped kitchen, electricity, and running water. It consisted of two floors, connected by an angular staircase leading to two miniscule bedrooms upstairs. The little house had miraculously materialized in our yard one January 6th on Three Kings Day, which Latins celebrate in a fashion similar to Christmas.

I loved the dollhouse. Before the revolution, I spent most of my free time playing in it. I prepared innumerable meals for parties whose guests were my imaginary playmates and dolls of porcelain and cloth. I was mistress of a household where the outside world had no place. It was a sacrosanct haven that adult realities could not penetrate.

When provisions began to become scarce, Dad had an ingenious idea. Once, after spending a day in the country, he sheepishly returned with a car full of squawking chickens. Laughingly, he asked my mother to meet him outside at the dollhouse and to bring him some of his tools. He took me aside and apologetically attempted to explain what he was about to do. "I'm sorry, Marcia, but you must lend us the dollhouse. I promise that one day you'll get it back. We are now going to begin raising some of the food that we need."

The full meaning of his statement made no real impact

36

on me. Not until I saw my parents diligently at work converting the dollhouse into a modified chicken coup did I realize my father's intentions.

For some time I persisted in futile, wistful attempts to preserve some semblance of order in the little house. I methodically disposed of feathers and broken eggshells which collected on the floor and clung to the curtains like medals awarded in a war conducted without opposition. One day I just quit going out there. I never played in the dollhouse again. Eventually, my father was forced to give up on his scheme. An ordinance was passed that prohibited people from raising animals for consumption even within the boundaries of their property.

Tata, our maid, was in the habit of taking me with her for daily walks in the afternoons after school. I enjoyed these outings tremendously, as we tended to venture into areas I rarely frequented otherwise. I particularly enjoyed lengthy walks in the Miramar district, where the majority of the foreign embassies were located and where landscaped lawns and lush vegetation gave the area an almost fairy-tale atmosphere. Stately mansions were interspersed among indolent palm trees, elaborate fountains, and an abundance of bougainvillaeas, hibiscuses, and gardenias. Its peaceful atmosphere was occasionally disrupted by cries from the many tropical birds that fed beneath skies resembling the inside of abalone shells. Strollers in linen *guayaberas* walked past us, amiably calling out greetings and tipping their beige panama hats.

We always culminated our walks at one of the many small sidewalk cafes that dotted the fringes of the district. Here we ordered dark, thick *maltas* or *batidos de fruta*, fruit milk shakes of papaya, tamarind, or mamey.

One afternoon on our walk we encountered a milkman

milkman

who appeared from a distance to be arguing with one of the embassy guards. Militiamen had by then been positioned outside all embassies in order to prevent unauthorized entrance. As we approached the quarreling men, it became evident that the milkman was being prevented from delivering a carton full of dairy products. Beads of perspiration began to form on the deliveryman's forehead and upper lip as he glanced longingly at the gates, which were slightly ajar. The guard was adamant. He argued that a routine delivery had already taken place during the morning shift, and that he was not authorized to allow another order in, even if replenishments were needed for that night's party.

Suddenly the milkman broke loose from the guard's firm grip and clumsily stumbled in the direction of the gate. He regained his balance and ran toward the driveway. The first bullet from the guard's rifle must have hit the man's left leg, as he shifted the bulk of his weight to his right and continued running. There followed a series of shots which perforated the man's back. One of them must have struck the nape of his neck, as the man's head jerked backward, almost touching his spine. Finally he fell and lay immobile among broken milk bottles and containers of melting butter and cottage cheese.

Screaming, Tata took hold of me and attempted to cover my eyes with the palms of her hands. She ran onto the street away from the line of fire, dragging me behind her. Mesmerized by the man's open eyes—by his lifeless, blank stare—I could not look away. His blood mingled with the spilt milk, soaking his white uniform pink. I remember noting the enormousness of the black bullet holes, aware for the first time of the discrepancy between bullet size and actual wound.

Apparently, the dead man had masqueraded as a delivery boy with the intention of reaching the sanctity of the em-

38

bassy. Its diplomatic immunity would have provided him with either temporary shelter or a safe conduct out of the country.

Many individuals persecuted by the regime for rebelling against the new social order had begun to flock to the safety of the embassies. With all legal avenues for emigration closed to them, many individuals devised ingenious methods to obtain political asylum. A great number of men have lost their lives while attempting to reach embassy grounds in Cuba. Some would climb over the barbed-wire fences during the night, unaware of the hidden presence of armed guards instructed and fanatically willing to fire at the slightest provocation.

I can still vividly recall the vacant look on the milkman's face. My very impressionable age didn't allow me to forget the incident. I dwelled on it for days, on every second of the man's painful, slow-motion trajectory from bewilderment to rage, to pain, and finally to death.

One April day in 1961 loud, insistent knocks at the door interrupted us during our evening meal. Mami cautiously opened the door and confronted Mario, the eldest son of old family friends. Mario was covered with mud and had deep slashes on his face and arms, which appeared to have been caused by a razor-sharp object.

"I must talk to Manuel," he said. His words were barely audible, and his handsome face was extremely pale. My father approached the bleeding young man and, recognizing him, helped him into the living room. Dad then stepped outside and casually circled the house, stopping occasionally to pull out a weed or pick up a toy that I had carelessly left outdoors. Cautiously, he made certain that Mario had not been followed. He then lit a cigar and returned to the house. Once the door closed behind him, Dad ran over to Mario and

39

asked him what had gone wrong. By this time my mother had begun to clean his cuts and had provided him with one of my father's clean shirts. I remember my momentary amusement at the shirt's ill fit.

"I must get away. I have no one to turn to. Our leader has been held for four days by the G2 and he has finally broken down."

My father asked him with equanimity how he had gotten hurt. "Jose confessed and turned our names in. I don't know what's going to happen to him. God help the poor devil, they've pulled out all his nails and beaten him up bad."

It seemed as if Mario kept swallowing nonexistent gulps of saliva over and over again as he spoke. Dad went over to the bar, poured some rum into a tall glass, and handed it silently to Mario, who took a large drink before speaking again.

"I've got to get to Marianao and warn the others. The G2 came by my place. I saw them coming, so I got away by breaking out through the kitchen window. That's how I cut myself. I came here directly, across the vacant lots in back, avoiding the well-lit streets. I really don't think I've been followed."

It was common knowledge among the neighbors that Mario and some of his friends, all law students at the university, had become increasingly angry about the atrocities being daily committed at the Cabana, a maximum-security prison on the outskirts of Havana. Their disappointment in Castro and their idealism had led them to plan and attempt a series of amateurish acts of sabotage. Their poorly executed plots had never really gotten off the ground. However, Jose Herrera, the clan's leader, had boasted of his group's courage while drunk at a gathering. Understandably, he had been picked up two days later by the G2 police.

As Mario spoke, it became evident that his first concern

was for the uncertain fate of his family. Retaliations against family members of escapees were a common occurrence, and Mario wanted my father to warn his parents and tell them that he was going temporarily into hiding. Dad withdrew his car keys from his pants pocket, stating that he was willing to drive Mario wherever he wished to go. Mom vehemently objected to Dad's becoming involved. He had already begun to receive intimidating telephone calls in which unfamiliar voices accused him of being a *gusano* and threatened to dispose of him. The word *gusano* is a common derogatory term in Cuba. Its literal meaning is "worm," and it was regularly used to describe a person disloyal to the state.

A plan was finally formulated and agreed upon that my parents hoped would get Mario safely to Marianao. Mother and I were to drive Mario to his destination in order to arouse less suspicion. We adjourned to the garage, and Mario hid in the trunk of the car, his body concealed by blankets and old rags. Dad gave us precise directions, and we climbed onto the front seat and drove away. A few minutes out of the Nautico area, we encountered a roadblock. Each car ahead of us was being systematically and thoroughly searched. We turned off the engine and calmly awaited our turn. A dark-skinned man with an unkempt beard approached our car.

"Pull over. Our orders are to search every car leaving the Nautico district. A gusano is being hunted down all over the area."

I have never been as proud of my mother as I was that day. Feigning great indignation, she identified herself and gave my uncle Jorge's name as a reference. At the time, my uncle was highly esteemed in government circles as a man whose patriotism and loyalty to Castro were beyond doubt.

The bearded man called his partner over to the curb where we were parked. I thought of Mario, lying defenselessly inside our trunk, his fate being decided by the outcome of my

41

mother's bravado. The two men were frowning and glancing uneasily at us and at each other. Our identification papers were in perfect order, and it would not do to humiliate such an esteemed man's sister in this manner. Such a mistake could be serious, especially given Jorge's excitable nature.

Detecting the soldiers' uncertainty, my mother interjected that I had not been feeling well all day. I was sick with a high fever, and she wanted to get me to a doctor as soon as possible. Her argument, impassively delivered, convinced the ambivalent men. Their roles shifted from prosecutors to protectors of an obviously innocent woman and her sickly child. Since the long line of cars waiting to be searched barred the smooth and rapid flow of traffic, the bearded man gallantly volunteered to escort us by motorcycle toward our destination. For several tense miles, the two of us and the unsuspecting Mario, still in hiding, were regally escorted south toward Marianao.

Conditions continued on a path of deterioration. The rapid innovations in policies and legislation affected even the nonpolitical segment of the population. Prior to Castro, you could smugly retreat behind your apolitical orientation. The changes implemented no longer made allowances for such rationalizations. You were inevitably affected by the very nature of the changes.

In hushed tones, inside rooms with dimmed lights, people discussed the fundamental differences between present and past governments. Cubans had faced before the necessity of removing egomaniac despots driven to power by self-interest and greed. But the current situation was different and required different remedies. Our present dictator was promulgating a little-understood ideology, modified somewhat to suit the island. Dissenters found themselves traveling uncharted waters—leaderless, bewildered, and afraid. Cuban society was being drastically altered, transformed through rhetoric and intimidation from a long-standing system based on private enterprise into a centralized, state-controlled economy.

All businesses were expropriated. Prior owners could request to remain as administrators, but approval was dependent on the extent to which they "proved" their loyalty to the new regime. Set salaries were assigned when the requests were approved. All business transactions were regulated; all money had to be accounted for. Business overseers were usually inexperienced individuals chosen as a result of party affiliation or nepotism.

Seizures continued indefinitely under Revolutionary Law 851, which had established the legal basis for the general nationalization of both Cuban and American property. If you had owned a car prior to the new regime, you were magnanimously allowed to keep it for private use as long as you did not try to sell it. Only government personnel were given access to the small number of imported models arriving on the island after the revolution.

Eventually, a Sunday morning Volunteer Activities system was established. All adults in good health were requested to "volunteer" a few unpaid hours on Sunday mornings towards the "betterment of the general welfare." People were forced to work in the sugar fields and in numerous civic projects chosen by the ever-growing bureaucracy. The custom of spending Sundays at home with your family was obliterated. Before the new law, Sundays had usually been reserved for *perniles de familia*; fires were kindled, deep pits dug in the ground, and enormous pigs roasted and consumed. Even Grandfather, by then in his seventies, was not exempt from the ordinance. The "volunteers" were herded onto trucks like cattle and sent off to their various assignments. A

43

government-instituted choteo usually accompanied them on their labors: *"Somos comunistas, pa alante, pa alante, y al que no le guste que se tome un purgante."* ("We are communists, let's move forward, let's move forward, whoever disagrees with us will be given a purgative.")

A riot instigated in Camaguey by the farmers to protest the forced sale of their products at government prices was instantly squelched. They had also been protesting the mandatory inventory of all farm animals. An inventoried pig killed by its owner for private use resulted in the owner's automatic sentencing.

Certain people were once again being exempted from justice. If a citizen committed murder and got caught, the courts tended to deal with him as if he were a common criminal. If the murderer was a party member in good standing, a more benign attempt was made to "rehabilitate" him through counseling and assignment to a work detail.

Prostitution had always been prevalent in Cuba. Prostitutes were now seen as victims of a previously sick society and were also rehabilitated through "volunteer" work in the fields.

"Micro-brigades" were instituted in which workers with little construction experience were charged with the task of building housing units for country families in need of homes. Understandably, the quality of the units was substandard, given the workers' lack of either experience or motivation. I know a shoemaker who was assigned to a construction brigade.

Apolitical artistic performances began to be viewed as endeavors that detracted from true revolutionary concerns. Once, however, a local dance troupe had to perform a classical ballet in honor of a visiting Soviet dignitary. My family attended one of the performances one evening late in May. We were embarrassed for the performers—sweaty, earthy,

44

voluptuous women clumsily trying to execute a Russian ballet. The precision of the dancers' *pas de deux* contrasted humorously with their evident desire to discard their stiff tutus and toe shoes and break into their dances of old.

Radio and television stations continued to operate, but broadcasts were increasingly used to indoctrinate rather than to entertain. All programs either contained political innuendoes or were themselves parables of an ideological nature. Children's programs were most blatantly affected, with the government actively promoting through them the direct ideological instruction of youngsters. My family, leery of the probable effect of such biased teachings, began to review all programs and selectively curb my exposure to them.

By this time, the realities of the new decrees were resulting in mass panic. People were extremely suspicious of each other. You never knew whether a friend felt a greater alliance to the state than to you and whether this alliance would result in his reporting you to the Committee for the Defense of the Revolution. The openness and trust that had characterized human relations among Cubans were no longer evident.

We all knew that the family living next door was hiding a "gusano" that the G2 was looking for. He never left the back room of the house in which he stayed, but we could see him through the windows, pacing the floor like a caged animal. It was common knowledge that he had been there in hiding for over two months. His wife, under the pretext of visiting friends in that house, frequently came to see him.

Someone must have reported to the authorities that he was there. They came for him one afternoon and dragged him away screaming. All the neighborhood kids watched while sitting on the curb of the sidewalk. When he struggled, the officers hit him hard in the stomach with the butts

45

of their rifles, and he collapsed. They hauled him away. We never saw him again. His wife went to visit him in jail. She came back saying that no one had gotten him a doctor and that she could see little white worms wriggling within his open wounds.

One night we received a visit from Jose, a good friend of Dad's. Jose told us that he needed to hide his brother from the G2 for a few days, and that Dad was the only one he could turn to. The brother would have to stay with us only until Jose could arrange for him to be picked up by boat. Then all Dad had to do was to turn the living room light on and off a couple of times. The boat would dock by the rocks in front of our house, and Jose's brother would quickly run in its direction. Dad agreed to help.

He killed a turkey he'd been keeping in my dollhouse for fear it would make a lot of noise. He thought he might be forced to hide the man in the dollhouse, and the turkey could give him away.

On the night the man was to be brought to stay with us, Dad noticed an unusual phenomenon. All the street lights on our block were off except the one exactly in front of our house. Dad called the electric company to inquire about what had happened. Dissatisfied with the explanation, he called Jose. Jose suggested that it might be best if his brother were gotten off the island another way. Later we heard that he had escaped by boat from Santa Clara province and that he eventually made it to Miami.

Two days later a policeman came to our house and asked that he be allowed to speak to Señor Manuel Fuentes. Trying to conceal her fright, Mom went and got Dad, who had been doing some paper work in his study.

"What seems to be the problem, officer?" Dad calmly asked the man.

"Señor Fuentes, you are requested not to play dominoes or

46

cards on your porch anymore," said the policeman firmly.
Dad had been in the habit of holding card and domino parties on the porch for years. He asked the government man why he was suddenly forbidden to do so.

"We believe that your parties are only an excuse for the neighborhood gusanos to meet and plan counterrevolutionary activities."

Dad was furious. He could not even get together with his friends and play cards anymore! The officer was adamant, so Dad's weekly get-togethers were not held again.

Then Mom became involved in the sale of *bonos*. Bonos looked like theater tickets and sold for five, ten, and twenty-five pesos. The money obtained from their sale was sent to the various underground organizations that conducted covert activities against the regime. Selling bonos was mainly something in which housewives were involved.

Mom got an anonymous phone call one afternoon. The woman on the line refused to identify herself. All she said was that she herself was a gusana and that my mother's involvement in the sale of bonos was getting to be common knowledge. "Be careful. Take it from a friend," said the voice. Mother tore up all her bonos and never sold any again.

Shortages continued to get worse. Families began to get rid of their domestic animals. People rarely kept pets anymore. Food was so scarce that people couldn't afford the luxury of keeping an animal at home. We were forced to put our dog to sleep because there wasn't enough to feed him. Trying to get enough to eat became the national sport.

Restaurants still operated. You arrived and were cordially seated at a beautifully set table. An extensive menu was handed to you. Once you were ready to order, the waiter calmly told you that the only dish available that day was fish or rice and beans, or whatever. A friend of mine ate so much rice to the exclusion of all other food while in Cuba that the sight of any dish made of rice now makes her nauseous.

The black market played an important role in the lives of the people. There one could pay as much as three hundred pesos for a pig, and as much as fifty pesos for a pound of ham or a bit of butter. Butter became so scarce that people resorted to making it at home. It was considered a luxury item. It was as scarce as chocolates or deodorant. A cousin of my mother's became so adept at concocting homemade deodorant that she supplied her whole block. Aunt Olga once got hold of a large amount of real butter. The sight of that smooth and golden substance made the members of her family look forward to supper as they had not been able to for a good while. The telephone rang during the meal, so Olga excused herself from the table and went to answer it. Upon her return, she found my cousin Roberto crouching like a dog beneath the table. He had discarded his silverware and was cramming the precious butter into his mouth by the handful.

People had to be very careful not to get caught using products available only through the black market. Marta, a friend of ours, was sent to jail for using black market cooking oil at home. Her daughter had reported her to the school authorities after being given a lesson on the evils and illegality of using black market products. The little girl was a very good citizen. By informing on her mother, she proved her great love for the state.

3

WHILE THE UNITED STATES
State Department criticized Castro's new trade arrangements
with the Soviet Union, officials secretly began planning to
train and equip Cuban exiles for an invasion of the island. In
January, 1961, the new president, John F. Kennedy, in-
herited the invasion plans prepared during the Eisenhower
administration. The invasion team, which had been training
in Central America, was ready to strike. Everything, however, went wrong from the beginning. The anti-Castro underground had been infiltrated, and Castro knew all about
the planned attack. His air force survived a pre-invasion
sabotage attempt, and once the exiles reached the beaches at
the Bay of Pigs, they were stranded. The arms shipped never
arrived. The air support assured by the American government was canceled at the last minute. American reinforce-
ments were waiting a few miles outside Cuban waters, but
at the last minute an order was issued that halted further aid.
Innumerable men died or were maimed at the Bay of Pigs—
young men, courageous, hopeful, trusting men whose only
mistake was that they were unable to believe in the retract-
ability of a promise.

Juan Fernandez is now thirty-eight years old. Prior to
participating in the invasion of Cuba, he was studying den-
tistry at the University of Miami and working part-time as

49

a gas station attendant. He was engaged to marry a young schoolteacher. His great love was sports, particularly water skiing. He does not ski anymore. He lost both his legs at the Bay of Pigs. They were amputated a few inches above his knees. He is back in Florida right now. He doesn't talk much, but his mother tells us that he is doing better. His naïveté led him to believe that he was to play an integral part in Cuba's liberation. Before he left for the Bay of Pigs, he told his girl that with the Americans on their side, how could they lose? He had cut out a picture of John F. Kennedy from an old magazine and hung it above the sofa in his living room. When he got back to Miami, he tore his cherished photograph of Kennedy to shreds.

He told me last year that at the Bay of Pigs he had scanned the skies, looking for the promised American help that never came. "Your men will handle the land operation and we'll take care of the air," he had been told.

"Whatever happened with the Yankees?" he asked me, looking puzzled.

Few people in Cuba were even aware that an invasion was taking place. Marcos Otero found out when he hailed a bus on Route 20 and found it full of prisoners bound for jail.

My uncle Rafael was a lawyer in Cuba. The morning of the invasion, he went as usual to a hearing at the Palace of Justice. Around ten o'clock a rumor began to circulate that an invasion was taking place. He disregarded the rumor, as many unfounded ones always seemed to be going around in those days. The radio had not made a definitive statement regarding an invasion. Broadcasts concentrated instead on reporting the details of an air raid two days before on the military camp in Marianao. At lunchtime, while leaving his office, my uncle was approached by two militiamen who asked him to identify himself. When he had done so, he was summarily arrested and taken to the basement of the Supreme Court building. There he found an assortment of judges, magistrates, attorneys, and legal clerks imprisoned. Like the others, he was shoved into a makeshift cell without an explanation. He remained there all night without being allowed to notify anyone as to his whereabouts. Prisoners were continually being brought in. At six o'clock the following morning, he and the others were forcefully taken by truck to the Castillo del Principe prison. The trucks were so tightly packed that a number of men died from lack of oxygen before getting there.

At the prison they were conducted to a communal subterranean cell—a large, dirt-floored pit. All the while, the militiamen taunted them about being gusanos and assured them that they were soon to be mercilessly shot.

The pit was dark and so humid that drops of water lined the walls. About six hundred persons were stuffed into an area with an actual capacity of about two hundred. It was so crowded that no one could move about freely or lie down on the floor to rest. The prisoners took turns sitting or standing up. Both men and women remained tightly packed inside the cramped area with no access to either bathroom facilities or running water. Individuals were forced to defecate on the ground. The stench was unbearable. The scraps of food occasionally thrown into the pit fell onto the excrement and were therefore inedible. The militia occasionally fired their guns in the air in order to frighten the prisoners. People hurled themselves on top of each other on the floor whenever the shooting began.

Some of the female prisoners were having their menstrual periods. To ease their predicament, several men tore their shirts to shreds and allowed the women to use them as sanitary napkins.

Once a day the guards stuck a hose between two of the

metal bars at the entrance of the pit and sprayed the prisoners with water. The thirsty mob always threw themselves at the bars, fighting wildly to get close enough to catch in their cupped hands a swallow of water to drink. My uncle frequently remained propped against one of the walls, fearful of being trampled. Occasionally, the guards sadistically turned off the water whenever a particular prisoner appeared to be satiating his thirst. After about twenty minutes had elapsed, the hose would be withdrawn, and there would be no more water until the following day.

Uncle Rafael worried less about his uncertain fate than about the effect of his imprisonment on my aunt. She could not know what had happened to him, whether he was alive or dead. Meanwhile, the possibility that my aunt herself might also be in jail caused him constant agony.

On the third day, the prisoners were given something to eat—a foul-smelling, gelatinous concoction in a rusty can. By this time, my uncle's hunger was so great that he felt that if he held his breath and quickly drank the mixture, he could keep it down. When he introduced the first spoonful into his mouth, the flavor was so putrid that he began to dry heave and then to vomit. Another one of the prisoners, a law clerk at the Palace of Justice, happened to be standing next to him. Aware of my uncle's revulsion at the ration for the day, he began to cry and to beg my uncle between sobs to allow him to have it. Rafael passed his portion to him. Before the young man could consume it, the guard on duty called out for the two of them to approach the bars. He asked Uncle Rafael if the soup was not to his liking. When my uncle acknowledged that he was unable to eat such a meal, the guard grabbed the can and poured its contents slowly onto the floor. He smiled while the young man begged to be allowed to have it instead.

A common form of torture at the prison was to place the

men that misbehaved in a metal container of sorts half-filled with water. The prisoners were made to stand inside the container for days at a time. They were unable to move about. Their legs swelled, and the water made the skin below their waist peel off and crinkle like tissue paper. The water mixed with urine and gave off an unbearable smell. Uncle Rafael and the rest of the men constantly dreaded the possibility that they might be sent to "the tube."

In jail, my uncle became friendly with an elderly Catholic priest from Spain. He was a professor at the Belén School, where he had taught Fidel Castro for many years. In their conversations, the priest said that he had been detained at his church along with its other ministers. During his captivity, he tried to contact Castro in the hope that their past relationship would result in his immediate release. Confident about his own innocence and counting on his friendship with Fidel, he patiently awaited the end of his imprisonment. One day a guard entered the pit and called out his name. Smiling, the priest raised his arm in expectation of an apology. Instead, the guard spit on his face and kicked him mercilessly until he lay bleeding and beaten to a pulp.

"Old man, you are a symbol of all that Fidel is trying to obliterate," said the guard as he left.

The old man lay silent, astonishment and pain on his face. Rafael approached him and nestled the old man's head on his lap. The man lay shivering, so Rafael took off his own coat and covered him. When the priest was able to speak, he softly told the prisoners of his experiences in Madrid during the Spanish Civil War. He said that when the fall of Madrid was imminent, the Spanish Communists had reacted as the Castroites were now reacting. Rounding up a mixed assortment of civilians whom they considered potential security risks, they had packed the country's jails with more than twenty-five thousand individuals. When Franco came into power, he found about twenty thousand persons who during the last days of the resistance had been methodically machine-gunned down in their cells by their captors. The priest implored the prisoners to pray that the invaders not capture Havana. If their liberators were successful, he insisted, their own fate would be certain death.

In order to prove his hypothesis, he instructed the men to contemplate a sight that had been worrying him daily. Through a crack in a wall, he directed the prisoners to look at the large number of machine guns and the ammunition readied as if in expectation of an imminent bloodbath. He recalled for them Castro's very words at a recent press conference where he assured the listeners that a successful invasion would result in the unwarranted extermination of great numbers of prisoners of war.

Uncle Rafael no longer regarded his situation as a frightening and senseless mistake. He sensed his predicament to be the culmination of a series of incidents in which he had voiced his growing disappointment with the regime.

All the prisoners remained in confinement for a period of three weeks. To the family members waiting outside the gates for his release, Rafael was unrecognizable when he got out. He had lost almost thirty pounds and for weeks was barely able to speak above a whisper. Yet compared with many others who were jailed during the early years of Castro's regime, he was lucky.

Celeste Campos is currently living in Puerto Rico. She was jailed as a political prisoner on November 22, 1960, and released in 1969. Celeste remained five years at a prison in Guanaja without being allowed to leave a small cell which she shared with six other women prisoners. There were over two thousand female prisoners in Guanaja, so arrangements were made to transport a few of the prisoners to Baracoa, in Oriente province. A new cell mate of Celeste's had recently given birth, in prison, to a daughter. Another prisoner, a midwife from Camaguey, had been brought into their cell at the last minute to assist during the delivery. On the morning of the transfer, Celeste, the prisoners who shared her cell, and a few hundred others were taken to Baracoa in armored cars. Their long journey along the Via Mulata was unbearably hot, and the newborn baby cried incessantly. Halfway to Baracoa, the caravan halted and the women were instructed to disembark. The new mother attempted to shield her baby from the sun while she breast-fed her. Three female guards approached the woman and removed the fidgety child from her arms. Celeste tells me that the woman is still in a Cuban prison and is unaware of her child's whereabouts. Her daughter must be grown now, if she is still alive.

The cells in Baracoa had neither running water nor electricity. The diet of the prisoners consisted primarily of bananas. Militiamen openly visited Baracoa during the night and forced themselves on the young female prisoners. Some of the women were as young as sixteen. Male guards treated their prisoners brutally, but female guards were even worse.

A favorite pastime at Baracoa consisted of rounding up some prisoners and enclosing them in a small outside corral. The guards would then hurl bottles filled with sand at them, the object of the game being to see how many prisoners could be hit within a predetermined period of time. Whenever one of the imprisoned women became seriously hurt as a result of the game, the guards assigned her care to one of the doctors or nurses who were themselves prisoners at Baracoa. Of course there was no suitable medical equipment or medication, so the mortality rate at Baracoa always remained high. Occasionally doctors would resort to such measures as sewing up wounds requiring stitches with common sewing thread.

The prisoners who had once supported Castro, but no longer did, were subjected to the most abuse. A young pregnant woman named Lydia, whose husband had been mortally wounded in an attempt to rescue her from Baracoa, was the most frequently maltreated. This young couple had been extremely active politically in the Sierra Maestra, dedicating themselves wholeheartedly to the overthrow of Fulgencio Batista. Then their gradual disenchantment with the new regime had led them to renewed political activity, only this time they were active in counterrevolutionary work against Fidel Castro. Their courageous pro-Castro stance had made them heroes to people of all ages. Their youth and genuine dedication to rectifying social injustice had captivated the imagination of the population. When they began to work against Castro, both were charged with sabotage. Lydia was captured when she was alone at home. Rogelio, her husband, came out of hiding and attempted, disguised as a militiaman, to rescue Lydia from Baracoa. His effort failed, and Lydia watched helplessly as her husband was shot to death. After his death was confirmed, Lydia became suicidal.

She often refused to eat, and would purposely take up the cause of every other prisoner against the militiawomen. Her belligerent attitude aroused rage in the guards. She was frequently beaten for her infractions, yet almost appeared to derive pleasure from her pain. It was as if suffering remained the only emotion that she could fully experience. During the summer, Lydia went into labor prematurely and died. Her child—a son—died as well.

Juana Pérez, a childhood friend of my mother's, was apprehended in a hospital the day after having a serious stomach operation. She was made to walk to the car and as a result hemorrhaged all the way to the prison. She was taken to the home of Pepe Rivero, which had been converted into a prison for political prisoners. There was no doctor available, so her fellow prisoners tried desperately to stop the bleeding and make her as comfortable as possible. They made bandages out of strips of bed sheets and nursed her even though she was unknown to any of them.

Juana's strong constitution allowed her to survive her ordeal. She recuperated slowly on the limited diet of rice. She was then transferred to Guanajay and finally to Guanabacoa, where she spent five years. At Guanabacoa, inmates were not allowed paper or writing materials, but they could have visitors once every three or four months. Visits were contingent upon good behavior, which often included submitting sexually to the guards. The women's husbands and children were allowed fifteen minutes during visiting periods, but they were strictly prohibited from expressing affection.

There was a guard at Guanabacoa nicknamed The Butcher, whose sole job was to correct the prisoners who disobeyed. The women assigned to her ranged in ages from sixteen to seventy-two. The Butcher was a tall, strong, robust woman who took sadistic pleasure in her work. Her favorite targets were young pregnant women. For some obscure reason these defenseless captives provoked within her the most savage rages. She was proud of the number of miscarriages she had induced, and savored the novel punitive techniques she frequently developed. The constant torment she inflicted on her wards resulted in a higher-than-usual incidence of suicide attempts at Guanabacoa.

Juana Perez once found her seventeen-year-old cell mate hanging by her belt from one of the ceiling's broken light fixtures. For two weeks prior to her suicide, the woman had

The Butcher guard ♀

been assigned to The Butcher's rehabilitative unit as punishment for hoarding scraps of food while on kitchen duty. She was kept naked in a cubicle about the size of an elevator and given no food for two weeks. The rat-infested cell had no lights or running water, and its stench was unbearable. The woman's only human contact during those two weeks had been The Butcher, who was seen daily entering and leaving the girl's cubicle, carrying brown paper bags which apparently contained instruments of torture. The sensitive young prisoner's subsequent suicide surprised few of the inmates. She was buried in a shallow, unmarked grave at Guanabacoa. Her family was not notified.

Most Cuban emigrants know many such prison stories. Their effect is ultimately numbing. Relatives and friends have witnessed and endured so much misery that ordinary social problems seem insignificant by comparison. So much is relative. For instance, it amuses me to read fiery articles about conditions in American prisons. It is impossible for me to listen to or read tales about the horrors of capitalism and American repression. I react with disdain at such naïveté, or with irritation at those who view social injustice from such a narrow perspective. I, too, am an American, but my own point of view is—different.

Eventually all private Catholic schools, including my own, were closed permanently by the government. Public-school attendance became mandatory. The Department of Education began the Promising Student Campaign. It consisted of the active recruitment of youngsters showing academic promise. Those students were then enrolled in special education programs and sent overseas, primarily to the Soviet Union, for training. A great many families were concerned about the Promising Student Campaign. Parental consent was not necessary for enrollment, and many parents feared

58

that their children, if chosen, would be taken permanently away from them. In retrospect, their fears were well founded. Many of the students participating in the program never returned to Cuba.

My parents chose to deal with this latest development by removing me from school. A physician and family friend sympathetic to their cause furnished me with the necessary documents for withdrawal. A fictitious disease was blamed for my inability to attend classes. A tutor, purely apolitical and dedicated only to the task of educating me academically, was hired. I was never to attend school in Cuba again.

My new teacher concentrated on having me learn English. This task I dreaded, fearing that I would never master its alien sounds and grammatical structure.

Señora Berta, overweight and always sweating profusely, arrived daily at the house, greeting me cheerfully with that most American of all greetings, "Hello."

"Hello, Marcia, how are you?"

"Hello, señora," I always answered sullenly.

I often attempted to procrastinate the inevitable lessons. Periodically, I asked why I was now forced to learn English to the exclusion of all other subjects. Berta, an elderly spinster who had once lived temporarily in the United States, would patiently repeat the litany—America was exciting, wonderful; I too might soon take a trip to America. I remained unimpressed. I was thirteen years old, totally unfamiliar with America and the English language, and I saw no value in pursuing such a boring course of study. I also missed attending classes at school. It was lonely without the presence of my classmates, and I longed to return to the school world that I had known before and loved.

Poor Berta tried hard to make the hated lessons relevant. She always brought along interesting pictures and toys, which she cunningly used to expand my vocabulary.

Mother, father, boy, girl, dog—I can vividly see myself fingering the little dolls, more concerned with their actual manipulation than with using them educationally. To me, America simply meant George Washington, the Empire State Building, and the Grand Canyon. A trip would accomplish nothing more than sightseeing, except maybe the satisfaction of a mild curiosity I had concerning the Americans themselves. Like many foreigners, I believed in the American mystique, the fantasies concerning Yankees—they are better fed, stronger, richer, taller. I also shared with the rest of the world a certain ambivalence toward the Yankees, a combination of awe and disdain, respect for Yankee technological prowess tinged with an underlying envy. Yankee accomplishments make one feel slightly and unpleasantly inadequate.

One cool, rainy evening in April, Tata came to my room with a message from my mother. "Niña, your mami wants to see you." My initial reaction was to wonder if she wanted to see me about my English lessons. On my way to the living room I prepared a slightly defensive speech describing my inherent lack of aptitude for the language. I was determined to tell her that if I indeed had to take language lessons, I would prefer to concentrate on French. I figured French resembled Spanish and would be easier for me to learn.

Both my parents were sitting on the couch, close to each other. I could see that Mami had been crying, as her eyes were red and puffy.

"Marcia, come and sit down. There's something we want to talk to you about," my father said softly.

I joined them, wondering to myself what had happened.

"You are going to take a trip to America."

"You mean, we all are taking a trip," I said, correcting him.

"No, only you and your mother."

"Why can't you come too? It sure would be more fun."
I was excited about the upcoming event but wanted Dad
to come with us.

Dad took my hand and held it gently.

"I can't, Marcia. I must look after the business," he said
firmly.

I couldn't wait until the following day to tell Berta that I
was finally going to America! Unable to understand my
mother's sadness, I ran to my room and picked up a book of
pictures entitled *The United States of America*.

"Don't be sad, Mami. Look, we're going to see the Empire
State Building!" I thrust the book at her so that she could
better appreciate what I was telling her. She only cried
harder.

"Don't cry," I told her. "We'll come back to Daddy real
soon, and we'll take lots of pictures."

Preparations for this particular trip were drastically different from all others. It seemed that I was the only one in
the house looking forward to it. Furthermore, I was told not
to say anything about the trip to anyone. Who had ever
heard of taking a vacation without telling a soul about it?

The atmosphere of fear throughout the neighborhood was
by now almost palpable. People who had been friendly and
hospitable before the revolution no longer invited you into
their homes. Friends of many years' standing made meager
excuses as to why they could no longer accept invitations,
even for dinner. People were terribly afraid. Their fear
arose from the awareness that no one, not even a child, could
be completely trusted.

The new regime initiated a grass-roots, neighborhood-
based program that efficiently detected all individuals criti-
cal of the government. A family was appointed on each
block to watch over the neighbors and report periodically
any unusual activity or suspected disloyalty. The system

worked extremely well. It minimized counterrevolutionary activities throughout the island, as no one individual could be certain of the extent or direction of another's loyalty.

An individual could obtain a number of greatly needed privileges depending on the number of families he periodically reported. The couple assigned this task on our block, Carmen and Diego Dominguez, had been friends of my parents for years. I once overheard a conversation between Carmen and my mother in which Carmen acknowledged her recent appointment and confidentially warned my mother to resist any temptation to become involved to any extent with the gusanos.

"I'm in a real bind, but it's better to be the watchdog than to be watched by dogs, no?" Carmen said, pressing her broad lips tightly together. "Diego's reasons are ideological, but I just want to be able to feed my kids properly."

My mother said nothing.

"When times are rough, you've got to think about yourself first, no?" It seemed as if she wanted my mother to condone her actions. "Look, I don't give a damn about the Martinezes or any of the others—or you, for that matter. Fidel made a lot of promises. So he kept some and not others. Don't deny it, you supported him at first and now you're disillusioned." Her tone was sarcastic.

"Yes, we supported him," my mother said cautiously. "We did more for Fidel than even you."

Carmen stood up and headed angrily for the door.

"I'm the loyal one now. I'm just warning you because I feel I owe it to you. Don't do anything foolish," she said.

Carmen and Diego Dominguez never visited my parents again.

The families that did continue to meet with us socially always had what seemed to me interminable conversations about the worsening situation on the island. Castro himself was such an enigma that people trying to understand him often traded anecdotes about him as a young man.

A man named Alejandro told the following stories to all those assembled at our house one Sunday afternoon. Alejandro, a high school teacher, had attended Belén High School with Fidel.

"One day during recess one of our teachers found him with a pocket knife carving his name on a young tree. The teacher called his attention to the fact that trees were good friends of man and that they ought to be preciously cared for, not destroyed. The following day when I arrived at the school, I found that overnight the tree had been mutilated. Suspecting young Fidel, the headmaster called him into his office. Fidel readily admitted that he had destroyed the tree and, smiling, said that he had done it out of vengeance as he hated to be scolded by anyone."

Alejandro continued his tale.

"Another time, Fidelito had an argument with a classmate. Another student came to me and told me that Fidel had produced a gun and that he said that he was going to shoot the other kid. He was fifteen years old at the time. Some of us intervened, taking the revolver away. He was so angry that he began to pound his head repeatedly against the cement wall of the schoolyard."

I helped Mom serve the guests while they debated heatedly among themselves how these stories could relate to Fidel Castro the adult. They feared him. They viewed him as unpredictable and longed to discover some characteristics that would help them predict his next move. It seemed to me that they were always wrong. Fidel always seemed to surprise them.

At these gatherings, another frequent topic of conversation was visas. Everyone spoke as if he had his own personal contact down at an embassy. For a fee, the rumor went, one could obtain an official-looking visa in a few weeks. Prices ranged from a few hundred dollars to several thousand. The amount depended on the number of documents that actually had to be forged.

I remember Alejandro making fun of those seriously considering leaving the country.

"So you think Fidel is really a communist?" He puffed on his cigar and laughed jovially.

"Fidel denied it at first, but now he freely admits it," someone said.

"You really think that the Yankees are going to allow communism on an island ninety miles away from the Florida Keys?" retorted Alejandro.

Some remained uneasy, but the majority, realizing the absurdity of the idea, joined in on Alejandro's contagious laughter.

Forgetting my mother's previous instructions, I began to tell our guests about our upcoming trip to America. My mother pinched me on my bare leg so harshly that I was black and blue for weeks.

After a few months of trying to get visas, people no longer expressed so much confidence in their ability to do so. People could get rich merely arranging meetings between prospective clients and corrupt government officials. It remained relatively easy for a woman to get a visa. She could always dispense sexual favors for that coveted piece of paper. I know a very attractive woman, married to a doctor, who had to sleep with over a dozen immigration officials before her family's visas were issued. As far as her husband knows, their visas were legally obtained. He is quite proud of the fact that he didn't have to bribe anyone financially to get out. The family is currently living in Miami. The wife told my mother once that she no longer enjoys sex.

Those unable to obtain the proper documentation began

64

to resort to illegal alternatives in order to leave the island. Their methods reflected their desperation; many chose to risk their lives for a chance to live freely and without fear. The majority attempted to reach America by sea, either on makeshift rafts or aboard inconspicuously small motorboats. Most were unsuccessful. Militiamen combed the shoreline daily, particularly the north side of the island, which conveniently faced the United States. The militia, utilizing both aircraft and powerfully swift motorboats, searched tirelessly for potential defectors. Early in the morning at the Malecon, Havana's main waterfront, as the sun and tide rose, the waves would hurl ashore the bloated, bullet-ridden bodies of men, women, and children who had tried to reach the Yankee mecca in vain. The militia would promptly gather up the bodies and take them away on trucks. None of these incidents ever received any news coverage.

All privately owned boats had by now been confiscated. Given their shortage, an increasing number of individuals attempted their escape by raft. These rafts were, for the most part, built of wood and tied together with rope. Large empty tanks were usually fastened on all four corners for buoyancy.

People usually left at night, rowing optimistically in the direction of America. Those few who did manage to slip by the ever-present militia usually died at sea from exposure or starvation. Incredibly, a number of them actually managed to reach Florida waters. Benito was one of the lucky ones. In his twenties at the time, he and three college friends were picked up by a cargo ship after their raft had been aimlessly floating at sea for seventeen days. They lived on only some water and a few candy bars. Ricardo, one of the young men with Benito, did not live long enough to be rescued. The rest, unwilling to dispose of their friend's body overboard, kept his remains on the raft. Benito's explanation was that they could not bear to see Ricardo's body devoured by the numerous sharks which perpetually circled the raft. Benito manages a record store in Tampa these days. He doesn't like to discuss his escape. He says that whenever he does, he dreams about it in vivid detail that very night. Last year he had a son. They named him Ricardo.

Whenever an escape was being formulated, those concerned were never quite certain that there might not be among them a member of the G2 secret police. Often members of the G2 infiltrated groups of potential gusanos, pretending to be gusanos themselves. The strength of their loyalty to the party transcended both friendship and family ties. Nothing took precedence over party loyalty. We know a woman who turned in her brother, as she felt him to be a potential threat to the regime. By this act her loyalty to the party stood unquestioned. He was sent to prison, and she was rewarded with a commendation and the accompanying social prestige. The brother's crime had been to offer his home as a refuge to a childhood friend involved in non-violent but nevertheless counterrevolutionary activities.

Once a G2 policeman had successfully infiltrated a group of gusanos and gained their confidence, he would tell them that he wanted to leave the island for political reasons. He would persuade them that he could somehow obtain a navigable boat. He would say that he knew a trustworthy fisherman who for a few thousand pesos could get them all safely to America. Enthusiastically, his victims would reply that their own families also wanted to leave the country. After a large enough number of people acknowledged their wish to leave, an evening would be set aside by the G2 member as the date of departure. Those assembled would be told to bring a sum of money with them, and to arrive separately at a predetermined location along the coast in order to arouse no suspicions. When all were gathered, they were told to await the boat that was due to arrive soon. Suddenly, armed men would surround them, shouting that all were under arrest.

In the confusion that followed, people often attempted to run away in all directions. Most would be gunned down. Whole families died in this manner. Those still alive would be detained and condemned to a minimum imprisonment of ten to twenty years. The money that the gusanos had brought along would be distributed among those responsible for the arrests, as a sign of appreciation by the government. I know of several individuals still serving time who were captured under these very circumstances. It was a common enough ploy.

Sometimes, the seamen on foreign merchant ships were responsible for escapes. Dalia Lopez and her two daughters, now living in New Jersey, became friendly with a Greek captain whose ship periodically docked in Matanzas Harbor. All three women, dressed in men's clothing, luckily managed to sneak aboard the Greek ship, where they were promptly hidden by the captain in a small compartment below deck. They remained in hiding and managed to survive without food or water and with very little air until the ship reached international waters. At the ship's next stop, the Canary Islands, the three of them formally requested political asylum. It was granted.

A man named Jorge ingeniously outfitted a raft that successfully carried him and his family directly to America. First he built the raft so that it would tolerate a great deal of weight. Then, he managed to secure an automobile to the top of the raft, adapting a boat's propeller so that it turned while connected to the motor of the car. This family arrived in the United States unharmed. You might have read this particular story in the newspapers. The American press was captivated by it.

Antonio, a second cousin of mine, decided to build himself a boat that would carry him to freedom. He and four friends worked on the project for months in his garage and constructed a makeshift launch that could be quickly assembled and disassembled. They bought a motor and a compass through the black market.

Daily, the group rehearsed assembling the craft, purposely in the dark, in order to simulate actual conditions. They perfected their procedure to a point where the craft could be made seaworthy in less than thirty minutes—the maximum time allowed by the circumstances of their escape. The cove they had chosen as the site of departure was surrounded by dark, massive boulders and thick foliage. Each night for almost forty minutes the patrolman under whose jurisdiction the cove fell was unable to guard it properly. For that short period of time his line of vision was completely blocked by the rocks and trees. Antonio and his friends planned to leave on a Friday night. That way they stood a better chance of being spotted in Florida waters, since fishing boats and pleasure yachts would be out.

Antonio came over for dinner one evening in February and over coffee told us how his plan was progressing. He expressed increasing doubts concerning the integrity of Gonzalo, one of his accomplices.

"This guy insists on knowing the date and hour of departure a few days before," he said frowning. "Don't you think it sounds a little suspicious, especially after we agreed not to know for each other's protection?"

After taking a drag on his cigarette, all my father said was, "Test him."

68

After discussing it with the others, Antonio told Gonzalo that he was canceling the escape, as he had serious doubts about its outcome. That very night, Antonio transported all of the boat parts to a friend's garage. Two days later the G2 presented themselves at Antonio's and asked to be shown the contents of his garage. Finding nothing, they searched his house and jailed him for a week, interrogating him brutally. They extracted all his nails with mechanics' tools and broke his arm in two places. Finally releasing him, they kept such a constant watch over him and his activities that Antonio gave up trying to escape. He remains in Cuba.

Mr. Martin, my uncle's next-door neighbor, became friendly with a man who confidentially told him that for a fee he could get him and his family out of Cuba aboard a foreign ship that regularly transacted business in Havana harbor. This ship would take them safely to America. According to Martin's source, the ship's captain could be bought for 5,000 pesos. Once the captain had been paid off, the Martins would be invited aboard to dine with him, where they would remain, in hiding, until the ship left the country on the following morning. Martin was told that his source was to receive ten percent of the bribe as a finder's fee. The date and time of departure were set. The Martins were instructed not to bring any luggage with them, so as not to arouse suspicion. On the way to the docks, the man asked Martin to hand over the money so that he could pay off the captain before they embarked. When they got to the docks, the man pointed out which specific ship was to take them to America. He told them to wait for about twenty minutes and then to approach the militia guarding that particular ship and say that the captain expected them for dinner. Martin was ecstatic. At the appointed time he and his family approached the armed men and told them what had been prearranged.

The Martin family was immediately arrested and taken by force to the offices of the G2, where an extensive interrogation began.

Martin's fourteen-year-old son had been told only that his father was a friend of the captain's. He believed that they had all been invited to dine with him. All that Mrs. Martin knew was that for a fee of 5,000 pesos the ship was to get them out of Cuba. Martin had been reluctant to disclose the plan fully to his wife and son for fear that they might unknowingly tell the wrong person. During their interrogation, which lasted two weeks, Martin maintained that he thought they were leaving the country legally. He told them that his contact had identified himself as a member of the G2 from the beginning. According to his story, the money was to go to the G2 committee fund, not to the ship's captain. His wife and son, also being interrogated, could neither confirm nor deny the story Martin was telling.

Martin was condemned to two years of imprisonment. His wife was placed under house arrest for the same amount of time. Whenever it was imperative that she leave the house, she had to request permission from her neighborhood's Committee on Vigilance. An individual on their block representing the committee was formally placed in charge of her case. Mrs. Martin died at home prior to the end of their sentence. Martin and his son were to leave Cuba later by other means.

People continued trying to get out of the country in whatever way they could. I know a family from Oriente who attempted to swim across Guantanamo Bay to freedom. One side of the bay is under Cuban control, while the other houses the Base of Guantanamo. The intervening body of murky water is many miles wide and constantly under surveillance by well-lit and fully armed glass-bottomed boats. Periodically, the guards fire onto the water, both to warn off potential escapees and to exterminate those who might have already ventured into the bay for the purpose of escaping. This family trained for their escape for months by swimming daily in rough ocean waters. One moonless night, the husband obtained an extremely long rope. He then drove his family to the Cuban sector of Guantanamo Bay and waited in the darkness for the area to be cleared of the occasional pedestrians who frequented it. He tied the rope around his wife's foot and, leaving room for them to swim, around one foot of each child and finally himself. He then coaxed his frightened family into the water. When they had been swimming only a short time, the youngest boy's leg cramped and he began to cry. He continued to swim for a few yards while holding on to his father, imploring him to turn back to land. The man finally cut the rope which joined him and his youngest son to the other children. He instructed his wife and the remaining children not to look back and told them to continue to swim across the swamp in a straight line. The man and his nine-year-old youngster returned to land, where the militia, having found the deserted car, were already looking for its owners. His wife and the other children made it to the safety of the base and are currently living in Miami. The man is still in one of Cuba's overcrowded jails, yet another nameless casualty of Castro's glorious revolution.

And then there was Carlos. Carlos tells his own story in two letters written to his cousin Rosa in Havana. The first one is dated February 7, 1971.

DEAR ROSA:

Sorry I haven't written sooner, but so much has happened, Rosa! I will tell you the whole truth. Mami and my brothers and sisters planned to leave Cuba and told me nothing till the last minute! I didn't want to go because my dog, Tico, couldn't come. I also didn't want to leave Grandma, who

71

Mami said was too old to come. They scared me into going because they told me that I would soon be eligible for the Young People's Military Service. You know what that means!

One night we walked for miles till we reached a swamp. We put our bathing suits on and after a while, we jumped into this muck. The water was so cold I could hardly breathe. In a while, the jellyfish started stinging us real bad. We swam and swam. We separated ourselves into two groups—Marta, Sandra, Felipe and Enriquito—Yoyi, Mami and me. My group was left a bit behind because fat Yoyi was getting tired. Rosa, the fish were jumping all around us, some hitting you in the face! Stupid Yoyi was getting real tired and afraid. She was swimming in circles and swallowing gulps of water. We were supposed to be swimming toward some lights in the distance, but we couldn't see them anymore. It was real dark all around, and bugs kept biting us in our faces. The current was very strong and Yoyi began to howl. Mami spotted a little key to our left and told us to swim to it. In a while we got to it. It was small with dry little plants that prickled our feet. It was real bad. I was swollen and purple from cold, and dumb Yoyi wouldn't shut up. Crying and shivering she was. The three of us spent the night there, huddled together, trying to keep warm. The next day it was worse. There were no trees in the key and the sun and bugs were awful! The plan was to try and figure out during the day which way to the lights. The lights were those of the Yankee base at Guantanamo. You know, people here in Santiago are always trying to get to it, but they usually get messed up trying. I had a fever and Yoyi got her period and was cranky, and we had round red bites all over. Mami was great trying to make us laugh, but it sure wasn't funny. When the sun was going down, these policemen on a motorboat saw us. They were very nice to us, making jokes. One of them gave Mami his shirt. They took us to the station, where they asked us all these stupid questions for two days. They wanted to know where Dad was. When we told them he'd been dead for a couple of years, they asked us who we wanted to call. Mami didn't want to get anybody into the mess so she said nobody. Anyway, they called Aunt Hilda (a mistake, you know how she is). They put Mami in this little cell and sent Yoyi and me home with Hilda. The whole of Santiago has found out. People are real nice, bringing us food and stuff, and proud that at least the others made it. Mami is in this jail for women that are no good. Her cell mate killed her four-year-old daughter by beating her up when she made her angry. After this, Mayito and his stepbrother tried to do like we did but they shot at them in the water. Things here are a real mess, so be glad you're in the Capital. Write soon, o.k.?

Love,

CARLITOS

The second letter is dated August 15, 1974.

DEAR ROSA:

It must surprise you to receive a letter from me at this time. I hope that you haven't forgotten your childhood buddy completely! I am now 15, and many things have happened since our "adventure." After Mami was put in jail, I didn't do very well mentally. Things got so bad that Aunt Hilda took me to a psychiatrist. He just made things worse, so after a while I ended up at the Centro Gallego for two months in their nut ward. When I left there, I felt a bit better. I was at least able to leave the house alone. Before, Rosita, I couldn't even bring myself to leave my room! I began to take showers every day (before I could only bring

73

myself to do it about once a month!), etc., etc., etc. I'd miss my family and would feel real down all the time. Dr. Vazquez is still seeing me regularly. He's a real nice man, Rosa. My life now is real regular. I visit with Juanito and Susana in Vista Alegre once in a while. Sometimes I feel fine, mostly I feel so depressed, lonely and miserable, I scare myself. I'm afraid that I have become a very strange young man. One thing that I do all the time is read. I read practically all day and night. It helps me. I am keeping a list and I have now read 311 books! Everybody is real happy in Miami. Marta married a Yankee and they live in Miami Beach. Sandra's got herself a job and is making good money. Felipe is going on with school at a special place for Cuban boys. For my birthday they all got together and called. The call finally came through at two o'clock in the morning. (You know how mean the operators can be, making nasty remarks and making people wait so long for calls from America!) Poor Enrique, I couldn't talk to. The government there sent him to a camp in Texas for psychiatric rehabilitation. I guess things really got to him, too.

Mami has not been doing very well. She's got some bad kidney problems and her asthma has gotten really bad.

Remember all the fun we used to have before, when we were all happy and together?

Your last letter made me feel real good. Please write again.

Love,
CARLOS

4

ONE FALL EVENING I WAS joined in my room by my parents as I was getting ready for bed.

"Marcia, sit down. We want to discuss something with you."

I remember climbing into bed and covering my feet with the blanket. My father remained standing while Mom sat on the bed facing me.

"The time has come for you to take your trip. But in order for you and Mom to get to go to America, you must first visit the island of Jamaica," my father said. "It's gotten very difficult to get U.S. visas, Marcia. The waiting lines at the embassy are as long as ten city blocks. Every day they get longer, and it's getting more and more difficult to obtain the proper papers."

I asked them why Jamaica in particular.

"Your father can get us visas to go there more easily. Once we arrive in Kingston, we can request the necessary papers to go to the United States."

"When do we leave?" I asked them.

"Next week."

"How long are we going for, Mami?"

"For a short while."

"Just so we're back in time for my birthday." I should have been suspicious that she didn't answer my question directly, but I was not. My birthday was in three weeks, and we had talked at length the week before about having a party for me complete with piñata and a roast outside in the yard. It was to be a good opportunity to get together with old classmates I hadn't seen in a long time.

After my parents left my room, I got out my atlas and studied the section on Jamaica. It was a British territory, I learned. I noted from the color photographs how similar to Cuba it seemed. Concluding that it would be a fun place to visit, I returned the book to its shelf and went to bed.

On the evening of September 10, 1962, my mother helped me pack my light blue weekend case. I casually selected a couple of dresses and a few pairs of slacks for the vacation. How thorough and meticulous my packing would have been if I had known that I was never to return to that room again! Toys, photographs, books, prized mementos—all were left behind. I thought I would be back in a few weeks. I have never gone back.

At times I have felt that there is no continuity to my existence, as if I have led two lives. One consists of those first thirteen years from which I have only memories, nothing tangible. I do not own anything that links me with that first life. Nothing that I cherished throughout those years can be found in my home. At times I feel that I was reborn at thirteen, when my second life began. My adjustment to the United States sometimes deludes me into thinking I have gone through a set of experiences similar to those of my peers. Sometimes, however, I feel like an amnesiac. Whenever slightly dated slang is used or a specific reference is made to something uniquely American or something in vogue prior to my arrival, I draw a blank. Howdy Doody, Groundhog Day, "Leave It to Beaver," southpaw, licorice,

The Wizard of Oz, Winnie the Pooh—all are foreign to me. They strike no familiar chords. I do not react to them, except vicariously. Fonzie raises no ghost of the '50s; I never fantasized about Elvis. Thanksgiving—What's Thanksgiving? I did not taste peanut butter until I was fourteen. Nevertheless, I share a sense of a native-American childhood which I never really experienced. It has been written on the tabula rasa of my mind by association with American friends, beside my memories of a childhood spent in Cuba.

I left in haste the house where I had grown up. I never even thought to glance back. My animals, toys, and belongings remained securely in my father's care. My clothes that needed washing, I put into the pink laundry hamper in the bathroom. My diary I left on the night table, the key hidden beneath my pillow. Letters, report cards, swimming medals, baby pictures, all were left behind. I locked the door to my room so Dad wouldn't be tempted to read the diary. I wonder if someone broke the door down or if it's all still as I remember it, if my bedroom slippers are still beneath my bed.

We drove all day to a town whose name I don't recall in the province of Camaguey. We spent the night in a small hotel named the Buena Ventura ("good fortune"), registered under assumed names. I thought at the time that the aliases were a joke my parents were playing between themselves.

The following morning we did not go downstairs to breakfast. Instead, my mother let down the hem of my dress. She produced numerous American dollars from her purse and began to sew them to my skirt, placing the bills between the folds of the hem. She told me not to say a word about the money to anyone, that she was doing it so that we could have some extra cash on hand. She also tried to stuff some more of the bills inside both our shoes, but desisted after I told her that I could not walk very well that way. She then pulled her hair back into a pony tail. Using bobby pins to secure the remaining dollars in place, she combed her hair around the money, creating a thick, fashionable bun. I was impressed at her dexterity. She sprayed hair spray on and, holding up a hand mirror, examined the back of her head in the bathroom mirror. Pleased with the results, she put the mirror down, smiled, and blew me a kiss.

We carried our suitcases downstairs, checked out, and drove in silence toward the Camaquey Airport. I was sitting on the back seat, trying to get used to my uncomfortably stiff skirt.

When we arrived at the airport, we saw a man being forcefully carried out of the main building by three militiamen. A woman, crying hysterically, followed them a few paces behind. The man's arm appeared red and swollen. Bits of plaster and dressings hung from his elbow and wrist. Rumors were circulating throughout the airport that he had unsuccessfully tried to conceal certain valuables within a fake arm cast. The militia had not been fooled. Shattering the plaster, they had found whatever was of value within. He would not make it out of the country now.

A great many individuals who were leaving the country legally resorted to concealing, in ingenious ways, money or valuable objects they wished to take out with them. One was always hearing tales about pieces of luggage with fake bottoms and hidden compartments. Shoe soles that came apart and concealed items of worth had become so popular that the G2 at Havana Airport make it a policy to check everyone's shoes before departure.

I noticed that my mother was wearing more jewelry than was usually her custom. She had also given me one of her gold bracelets to wear. It was too large for my wrist and kept slipping off my arm. At that time, travelers could still take with them some pieces of jewelry, as long as they were actually worn. Months later women leaving the island would resort to such methods as inserting them into their vaginas in order to get them out of the country. I was later to learn that all of our jewelry, regardless of its emotional value, was meant to be sold in America for money to live on.

We stood in lines for hours in order to be searched by the authorities. Dad was not allowed to enter the area reserved for those departing. We could see him chain-smoking through the glass pane. It was hot. The ceiling fan was not working. Impatiently, I moved away from the line and approached the glass pane in the hope of catching Dad's eye. As I drew near, I noticed something I had never witnessed before. My father's eyes were bloodshot from crying. I vividly remember how upset I became at that sight. Crying myself, I ran toward my mother announcing that I did not want to go on this hateful vacation without Dad. She slapped me across my face and shouted, "Enough of this!"

At that very moment a heavyset militiawoman with oily, unkempt hair announced that our turn was next. We followed her into a plywood cubicle that was furnished with only a table and chair. Sitting down, she began to fill out some forms.

"Purpose of your trip abroad?"

"Pleasure," replied my mother.

The woman looked up with disdain.

"Length of stay?"

"A few weeks."

"Empty your pockets and undress."

The abrupt manner in which we were asked to undress jolted the two of us. We made a pile of our clothing on the floor, Mami cautiously making certain that my skirt fell beneath her dress and my blouse. We finally stood in our shoes and underwear in front of the stranger.

79

"Take everything off."

"I really don't think this is necessary," Mami interjected.

"Do as I say if you want out, Gusana."

We meekly undressed and stood before her. She approached Mother and said, "Spread your legs."

I could see my mother holding back her tears while the woman searched her. Satisfied that we were concealing nothing, she told us to get out and wait for our flight to be called.

An elderly woman was brought in. She smiled at us warmly. Though we were strangers, the humiliation resulting from our identical predicament made us intimate allies, if only for that brief moment. As we were leaving the room, I turned back and saw her standing in her underwear, sensibly folding her clothes and resting them on the chair.

We had been able to purchase a nominal amount of British currency to be used during our stay in Jamaica. A friend of my father's already in the U.S. had deposited $400.00 in my mother's name in a Kingston bank. Jamaican officials required at this time that Cuban visitors have a set amount of cash available to them before entering their country. They were understandably protecting themselves. They did not want to be responsible for penniless tourists who might very well choose not to return to their homeland again.

Our flight was announced. We looked around futilely for Dad but couldn't spot him in the crowd. Unsuspectingly, we were on the threshold of a second life. This flight was about to transform us from private citizens into homeless immigrants. We were led aboard.

The flight was uneventful. Mother, although calm, looked longingly out the window for its duration. She declined my invitation to play cards. Unaware of the full impact of our trip, I amused myself by reading all the brochures on Jamaica that were available on the plane.

During our approach to Kingston, I was immediately impressed by its majestic terrain. Green mountains jutted out of the ocean, and I could see long stretches of white beach intermittently dotted with swimmers. The island looked like a paradise, beckoning us to partake of its loveliness and to bask in its sun. I was enchanted, impatient throughout the landing, customs, and luggage rituals. Outside the airport we encountered eager black hands that held out to us wooden necklaces and straw hats. I wanted to buy a pink conch shell that a little boy in rags thrust into my hands. I told Mom that Dad would like it very much, but she replied that we couldn't afford it. Her attitude struck me as unusual, since the shell sounded so inexpensive. We would surely have to buy a great many gifts for the family before going home.

Mother hailed a cab and gave the man a crumpled piece of paper with the words *Mimosa Manor* written on it in Dad's writing. Throughout the almost two-hour car ride, the man kept laughing to himself and talking incomprehensibly in English. We finally arrived at a small guesthouse nestled among the trees. The man kept saying, *"Trienta, trienta."* We understood him to be saying that the fare was $30 in American money. We paid him and he quickly drove away in a cloud of dust. We later realized that once the driver became aware that we knew no English and had never been to Kingston, he had unnecessarily driven us all around the city before taking us to our destination. The guesthouse was less than forty-five minutes from the airport. His ploy to take advantage of us had worked. This incident set a pattern that would persist for some time to come. We were easy targets in those days.

The Mimosa, built out of stone, had been constructed at the turn of the century to serve as a sugar mill. Later it had been transformed into a modest guesthouse by the family that now owned it. That very evening I took a long walk around the property, marveling at its unique flavor and at the unusual configuration of rectangles that comprised the main house. It was unlike any hotel I had ever stayed in or visited. Our room was located at the end of a long, dark corridor. Although small, it had beautifully polished wooden floors and high ceilings. Above the dresser there was a window which faced the rear garden. Instead of glass, the window was covered by thin iron bars. Delighted with our accommodations, I examined everything and remember running to the lobby the next morning so that I could get a postcard of the Mimosa to send to Dad.

The following Monday we began a daily routine which continued for almost four months. The bus route to both the Kingston government offices and the American embassy was traced on a map for us by the clerk at the hotel. We would awaken before seven in the morning and faithfully follow the directions to our destination. Our stay in Jamaica was now dictated by our unusual legal status. We required a transit permit, which was valid for only twenty-four hours. Thus we were faced with the task of renewing it daily until our American visas were in order. Every day we waited in line at the Jamaican offices in order to extend our stay in Kingston one more day. We then waited outside the American Embassy in order to ascertain whether our request for immigration had been approved.

The lines were long and the Jamaican sun shone mercilessly on us. It seemed as if there were only Cuban people waiting in those lines. Often, individuals recognized each other from home. They hugged, traded addresses, and joked about their similar predicaments.

Some of them, having run out of money, were sleeping on the back streets of Kingston. It seemed that the majority of the people there were women and children. It was as if a tacit agreement had been made by all husbands and fathers to remain in Cuba for as long as they could. One day, as we waited in line, a woman remarked about the phenomenon to my mother.

"Most of the men have grown to love the crops they raise and the businesses they run as much as they love us. They want us safe, but they also want to hold on as long as they can to the work that gives their lives meaning. That's how it is with my man."

Mami agreed with the woman and told her that it was also like that with Dad.

"My husband thinks that things are deteriorating so rapidly that it all can't last for more than a year. Why have what you've worked for all your life confiscated when Castro's regime is almost certain to end soon, no?"

This woman was encountering unusual problems in obtaining her visa. Her son was mentally retarded, and the authorities were expressing some reluctance to issue him his entrance papers. They had been living in the Jamaican limbo for almost six months.

That night Mother tried to explain to me as best she could our present circumstances. I was beginning to feel homesick, and dreaded the long daily waits. I was not to understand fully the magnitude of our predicament until months later. I clung tenaciously to the belief that things would soon be as they had been. All I knew was that I wanted to go home.

In order to save money, we got a small hot plate and began to buy canned goods, which we stored in the closet. Every evening we heated up our canned dinners in the room.

Before going to bed Mom always placed the few pieces of jewelry we had brought with us, as well as all her documents, in her brown leather purse. She then put the purse beneath her mattress. One night, after a particularly difficult day, Mom forgot to place our valuables beneath the mattress for safekeeping. We had mistakenly gotten off the bus at the wrong stop that day, and had wandered aimlessly through the back streets of Kingston unable to make ourselves understood. We couldn't find our way back to the guesthouse. A young student overheard us speaking Spanish to the passersby while trying to find a police officer or directions back to the Mimosa. Approaching us, he offered in Spanish to drive us back to our hotel. Originally from Santo Domingo, he was vacationing in Jamaica for the week.

After he kindly dropped us off at the Mimosa, we went directly to our room. Mom kicked off her shoes and went straight to bed and to sleep, carelessly leaving her purse on top of the dresser. In the middle of the night an unusual noise woke us up. We sat up in bed and saw Mom's purse suspended above our heads from a long, thin stick with a hooked end.

Mother reacted immediately. Jumping out of bed, she climbed up on top of the dresser and lunged for the purse.

"Marcia, go hide in the closet," she screamed in my direction.

Wide awake by now, I felt myself hypnotized by the sight of Mami in her nightgown savagely striking through the window bars at a man perched outside on a tree. I saw a large, dark hand covered with curly black hair fiercely grabbing at the purse through the window bars. With his other hand, the thief was trying to pull the wooden stick toward him. The stiff handle of the purse was still being held by the stick's curved tip. Mom, clutching at the purse, was screaming hysterically in Spanish.

Running into the closet, I lost my balance and fell to the floor. Our supply of canned goods tipped over and fell on top of me. I crouched in a corner of the closet, whimpering and hiding my face with my hands. Suddenly I heard a dull

84

thud, the sound of dead-heavy weight falling to the floor. Instinctively knowing that it was Mami, I ventured out of the closet.

My mother was lying very still on the floor. Above one eye she had a deep cut, which was bleeding profusely. Her nightgown was in shreds, and the wooden stick lay beside her on the floor. I could not see the man or the purse.

Crying, I sat down beside her and placed her head on my lap. She stirred. I ran on my bare feet down the corridor and across the courtyard, in the direction of the manager's room. Knocking forcefully on his door, I managed to waken him. Groggily, he opened the door. I grabbed his hand and, pointing in the direction of our room, cried out, "Come, come." How does one convey terror and need without knowing the words that give sentences their meaning? I began to tell him in Spanish what had happened. The irritation he felt at being awakened was evident in his expression of disgust. I finally convinced him by my gestures that he should follow me to our room.

We arrived to find Mami still unconscious. The man bent over her and said something with the word *doctor* in it. "Doctor" is said almost identically in Spanish, so I nodded that I understood his meaning.

By the time the doctor arrived, Mother had regained consciousness. She panicked when she realized that the purse was gone. She kept saying, "The papers, the papers," over and over again. The doctor tried to give her a sedative, but she refused to take it. He tended to the cut and examined her chest, where the man had struck her repeatedly while they fought. None of her ribs appeared to be broken. After regaining her composure, she requested that the police be notified.

"Policia," she said. That was also understood.

We spent the rest of the night at the Kingston Police Station trying unsuccessfully to explain the circumstances of the robbery and the contents of the purse. An interpreter was finally called in who helped us fill out the necessary forms. Our picture made the front page of the *Kingston Daily* the next morning, with me in my pajamas staring vacantly at the camera, Mom with her head covered with bandages, and our names misspelled.

Mother became convinced that it was a Castroite plot designed to get hold of the papers she was carrying. Apparently, if they fell into the wrong hands, Dad's freedom in Cuba would be jeopardized. She agonized over the situation for two days until the purse was found on a sidewalk a few miles from the Mimosa. The jewelry was gone, but the documents were found intact. She was finally convinced that the robbery was totally unrelated to the political situation we had left behind. Even so, the thought of that man keeping a nightly vigil on us from atop a tree was so distasteful that we decided to move out. As our resources had been nearly depleted by the robbery, we moved to the House of Britain, an inexpensive guesthouse that the Kingston Chief of Police helped us find.

The wait continued.

A Cuban exile, Dr. Cosme de la Torriente, arrived in Kingston from Miami to act as a spokesman for the large number of us that needed help so badly. He was very helpful and is dead now, so I am giving his real name. I guess it doesn't matter anymore. He met with a number of the families stranded in Kingston. Since he spoke English well, he became our advocate. He was instrumental in getting the U.S. Embassy to begin posting outside the lists of names of those whose papers had been approved. This procedure freed us from having to stand in line every day waiting to have an actual interview with the embassy personnel regarding the status of our visas. We had grown to dread those waits.

Well-organized groups of natives had begun to heckle us, spitting at us as we stood in line around the embassy and shouting, "*Putas, putas, vuelvanse a Cuba*" ("Whores, whores, go back to Cuba"). We never could figure out why they persisted in doing this.

After the lists of names began to be posted outside the building, a few Cuban families banded together to help one another. Each chose a particular weekday when they were to be responsible for checking for a number of names on the lists. The day assigned to us was Tuesday, so every Tuesday we went down and looked at the lists. The other days, we were free to stay at the hotel.

Everyone was eager to get to America. The majority planned to settle in Miami. Miami's close proximity to Cuba, its climate, and its already large Cuban population were the main reasons for the choice. Everyone seemed to have a relative already living in Miami. It also had a fairly well established refugee program designed to help the growing influx of exiles. Rumor had it that the Yankees there were sympathetic toward us and were welcoming us with open arms. One Wednesday afternoon we received a frantic call from Rodriga, whose day it was to check the lists. Our names were on that day's roll. Our joy knew no bounds! We treated ourselves to the luxury of a cab and rushed to the embassy, arriving just before it was ready to close for the day.

We were assigned an alien-registration card that we were told to carry with us at all times. We were also told that every January we had to report our whereabouts to the U.S. immigration officials, either by mail or by visiting any U.S. post office and filling out the appropriate form. We were each assigned a number. We no longer owned a passport.

87

Our Cuban passport became only a worthless memento. The man down at the embassy told us that if we ever wished to travel to a foreign country, we would need a visa and an American re-entry permit. After a period of five years, he said, we could choose to become American citizens. We barely listened to the translator as he related the process by which we could gain American citizenship.

In five years I'd be celebrating my eighteenth birthday at home! By then, this nightmare would be reduced to a series of humorous anecdotes we'd tell while sitting on our dear porch facing the sea.

5

TWO DAYS LATER WE AR-
rived in Florida for the first time. The moment we set foot
on the ground at Miami's international airport, we and all
the other Cubans aboard the plane were led to a spacious,
antiseptic waiting room. There, a freckled American who
spoke Spanish welcomed us warmly to the United States.
He then asked that all of us who had managed to leave our
country with falsified papers raise our hands. No one did.
Gently, he explained that those of us with false visas would
not be sent back to Cuba. According to him, the U.S. government merely needed this information for its files. After
his reassurance, about a dozen hesitant arms went up. Those
of us whose papers were in order were then allowed to leave
the waiting area.

Aunt Ramona was waiting for us outside the terminal.
My mother had told me while we were in Jamaica that we'd
be staying with Ramona for a while. She had been living
in Miami for over a year, supporting herself by working as
a seamstress. In the car on our way to her house, Ramona
pointed out to us with a wave of her fat hand areas of the
city that were part of the *Cubaneo*. In Miami, an area *del
Cubaneo* refers to a location with a high concentration of
Cubans. Miami is bloated with Cubaneos.

"Here you'll be able to get any *condimento* you need to cook the food we're used to," she said.

She went on to poke fun at the tasteless meals the Americans ate. Their food is plain, she told us, *"no salsa"* ("no sauce"). Ramona, wishing to dazzle us with her newly acquired English, laced her conversation with Yankee words we didn't understand. She said something about "hamburger" and grimaced. I didn't have the slightest notion then what she meant. Chewing madly on a piece of gum, she also said that people here ate at odd times—instead of having their main meal around two o'clock in the afternoon and a very light supper at nine, the Americans had a lunch at noon and ate their main meal around seven. She told us with pride how Americanized she had become and asked if we had noticed. We had noticed, all right. Ramona was wearing tight slacks and a bright pink blouse. She had dyed her curly black hair; it was now the color of wheat. She wore a thick medal of the Virgin of Caridad around her neck and a ring on just about every finger, and to us she looked ridiculous.

Shortly, we arrived at her small apartment in the northwest section of the city. Her sewing room was to become our bedroom. Ramona had borrowed two cots for us to use. They were propped against the wall amid yards of discarded material. A mannequin looked blankly at us through glass eyes as we undressed for the night.

The following morning Ramona took us on a tour of the city accompanied by her friend Bill, who ran a grocery store nearby. Bill did not speak any Spanish. He was blond, with a ruddy complexion and an enormous, protruding stomach. Its bulk kept causing his shirt to unbutton. Laughing, Ramona would occasionally insert her fingers through the opening in the shirt and tickle his stomach. He found her teasing extremely amusing. They giggled and between themselves spoke only in English. They drove us all around the Coral Gables section, where most of Ramona's clients lived.

"These gringa whores just want to take advantage of you," she said. "They eat in our restaurants, sleep with our men, and break down my door for me to sew for them, but at the same time they are wishing us a thousand miles away."

Mother tried to make herself useful at Ramona's by taking over the cooking and cleaning. That suited my aunt just fine. She began to stay in bed until noon, or until one of her clients showed up. Whenever one of them arrived, we evacuated the sewing room and Ramona ushered the woman in for a fitting. She once said that if there was ever any leftover material, she'd make me a dress. I had not brought any winter clothes with me, and it was cold. She never did.

Bill began to spend just about every night at the apartment. There was no door between the sewing room and the bedroom, so in order to have a little privacy we hung a few yards of cheap cloth from a curtain rod in the doorway. At night we could clearly hear Ramona and Bill making love in the next room. Their grunting and panting would awaken us, and we'd lie there with our eyes closed, pretending not to hear.

The first time we overheard them I sat up and asked Mami what was going on in Ramona's room. I first thought that someone must surely be sick or in need of help. Mother replied in a whisper that it was only the rats, and that I should just go back to sleep. I never asked again. Sometimes I awakened not from the sounds of sex, but from the muffled sobs of Mami lying beside me with her pillow over her head.

Ramona was very much involved in *Santerias*. Santeria is a combination of witchcraft and religion commonly practiced by Cubans, particularly among the lower classes. Adherents mix potions made from various herbs or animal blood and splash them on themselves for protection. All of Ramona's friends were always having *despojos* to undo the *maldiciones* ("curses") placed on them by their enemies. A *despojo* is somewhat similar to a seance, but the dead are not invoked. Instead, by participating in the ritual, the person rids himself of whatever evil may have been directed at him.

I always tried to stay up on the nights that I knew a despojo was to take place. I watched the goings-on from the sewing room through a tear in the cloth. The participants always lit candles for the occasion. Standing in a circle, they danced and shook to the rhythmic sounds of their clapping hands, groaning and singing obscure Spanish songs in a monotone. A friend of Ramona's, a black woman in her fifties, used to turn dead white during the trances she experienced at the despojos. Her eyes would roll back, and her lips would stand out dramatically, looking unusually full and purple against the white pallor of her face. The candles in front of Ramona's figurines of the Virgin of the Caridad and of Jesus and the Virgin Mary would glow eerily.

Ramona gave me an *asabache* once. Asabaches are shiny black stones that are said to have preventive and curative powers. People wear them concealed around their necks on a thin chain. They are said to be particularly effective when worn by children, pregnant women, and beautiful virgins. These susceptible people are frequently subject to the maldiciones of those less fortunate—the old, the barren, the ugly. Jealousy might even transform an intended compliment into an unintended curse. If an individual is protected by an asabache, she needn't worry; the conscious or unconscious maldicion will ricochet back to the sender.

Ramona put the asabache around my neck one afternoon while we drank tea together in the kitchen. She told me I must not tell my mother that she had given it to me. Mami was a disbeliever; the gift was to be our secret.

"One day you'll probably be very grateful that I took the time to watch out for your interests," she said confidentially, leaning towards me.

I still have the asabache. It looks infinitely smaller and less awesome to me now than it did on that day.

During the summer months I viewed our living in Miami as temporary—an unpleasant episode that would end when it was safe to return home. There were no books or magazines I could read or television programs I could watch and understand. The town was a Tower of Babel in which people made sounds with their mouths that I knew were fraught with meaning, but indecipherable meaning nevertheless.

I was lonely. I'd sit on Ramona's front steps, watching the neighbor's two daughters play and wanting very much to join them. Once, while happily jumping rope on the sidewalk, they noticed my presence. Approaching me with a smile, the elder girl said something to me that I didn't understand. I tried to communicate with her, but couldn't. Mother, father, water, hamburger . . . How did you say, "Do you want to play with me?" I tried hesitantly to make myself understood in Spanish. Their puzzled looks immediately told me that we would never share any of our thoughts, worries, or dreams. An impenetrable barrier stood between us, and we all sensed it. Giving up on me, the girl shrugged her shoulders and walked away. I became aware for the first time that my isolation was bound to perpetuate itself indefinitely. If I wanted friends, I'd have to apply myself seriously to learning this new language. Besides, the thought that I might have to attend classes under such conditions terrified me.

I began to have a recurring nightmare in which I'd see myself in a classroom with slender, blond students who joked and chatted among themselves in English. The teacher would direct a question at me and I'd ignore her, unaware that she was speaking to me. Jeering, my classmates would make me stand up and force me to speak. Whenever I uttered a sound, they'd point their fingers in my direction and laugh. The teacher would invariably end up laughing along with them. The dream haunted me so much that every night before falling asleep I'd pray for something to happen that would prevent me from starting school in the United States.

One day at the end of August, Mom decided that it would be best if the two of us moved to a place of our own. She pawned her watch, and we paid a month's rent of forty dollars for a room at the Marlin Guest House, a block from Ramona's. We bought two plates and some silverware, and transferred our single suitcase to the Marlin. We'd wash the dishes in the sink and our clothes in the bathtub. Having brought our secondhand gas burner with us from Jamaica, we continued to cook for ourselves in our room. We wanted to stretch the bit of money that we had left.

I knew that the manager—an old, bent man originally from Romania—felt really sorry for us. He suggested that Mami clean the halls and lobby of the guesthouse in exchange for our rent. Mami gratefully accepted. A friend of his owned a dilapidated old hotel three blocks from the Marlin. He worked it out so that Mami also got herself a part-time job there as a maid. I'd go over and help her do the cleaning two or three days a week. We'd do about thirty rooms on any given day, which meant we'd have twenty-five bathrooms to clean and forty or more beds to make. Mother in her white uniform and I clinging shyly to her skirt would walk afterwards slowly back home.

A woman named Lisa moved into the room next to ours at the Marlin. Lisa used to work as a salesgirl in Cuba at El Encanto, Havana's most exclusive department store. When

El Encanto was expropriated by the government, she and many of the workers decided to do away with the store. One afternoon at closing time, after ringing up her last sale, she put an explosive inside the pneumatic tube which, passing through every floor, carried the money from the sale up to the cash register on the top floor. El Encanto burned all night. Its destruction made Lisa happy. Another young saleswoman, however, was charged instead with the crime and executed. Lisa never forgave herself. She must have told me the story of El Encanto a hundred times. Whenever she was in a good mood, she'd picture herself as a heroine who had played a dramatic, praiseworthy role in the sabotage. Whenever she was depressed, she'd tell her story teary-eyed, labeling herself a murderess and condemning her act as reckless and insane. "My soul is doomed to burn in the Eternal Fire," she'd say.

Throughout this period, people at the Cuban Refugee Center helped us in as many ways as they could. We'd go there, and they'd give us anything from army surplus food rations to used clothes. Entire Cuban families flocked to the center during the fall to obtain whatever coats or sweaters could be spared. Small children kept warm by sitting on the floor between their mothers' legs while the women stood in line. There were large storage rooms filled with boxes containing old clothes donated by the charitable organizations and churches of the area.

The government also helped us with actual cash. We were grateful. Used to expecting nothing from the government, we marveled among ourselves at the numerous programs set up to help the needy in America.

A few years later, a Washington agency was to receive a check for a substantial amount of money from a group in Miami. A Cuban organization had started a city-wide collection in order to repay the Yankees for their kindness.

Many refugees looked on the financial help they'd received upon their arrival in the United States as a loan; now that the majority of them had jobs, they felt ready to pay back some of their debts.

In the fall Mami enrolled me at the Riverside Public School. I was assigned to a classroom where I was the only non-English-speaking child. Through an interpreter, my mother was told the potential benefits of such a placement. I would learn English faster, she was told, if I were to attend regular public school along with the other children in the neighborhood. According to their rationale, I would also quickly establish some friendships in the area.

The night before school was to begin, I tossed and turned in my bed all night, unable to fall asleep. What I'd been dreading was about to take place. While I longed for some companionship from the kids my age, I dreaded their possible rejection of me. When you're young, possibly your greatest need is to be liked by everyone. Any departure from the norm that points up your inherent alien status is dreadful. And I was different. I did not fit in.

I had gotten a pair of brown-and-white saddle oxfords from the caseworker assigned to us by the refugee center. As they were a few sizes too big, we stuffed the tips with tissue paper to give me a better fit. They made my feet appear slightly deformed and too large for the rest of my body.

How vividly I remember that first day—my too-large saddle oxfords, my skirt that was much too long, my agonized, shy nervousness. The experience was almost as bad as I had dreamed. I sat at my desk unable to understand either the teacher or my classmates. They all seemed to have known each other prior to the first day of school. They smirked among themselves, some openly laughing in my face while pointing at my shoes. When the teacher asked the boy sitting next to me a question, he answered her in a voice grotesquely accented. He rolled the *r*'s in his tongue as I did then. Everyone laughed.

The situation lasted exactly one week. I'd come into the classroom, sit down at my desk, and assume an expression designed to fool everyone into believing that I understood what was being said. No one was fooled. The teacher periodically asked questions, going down each row. When my turn came, she'd skip me, asking the girl behind me the question intended for me.

I sat alone to eat my lunch, which consisted of a hearty Cuban meal cooked by Mami with the best of intentions. No hamburger for me. On Thursday someone hid my lunch. Unable to find it or to ask the lunchroom staff for something else to eat, I sat at a table and silently watched my new classmates. I tried to enjoy vicariously some of the carefree exuberance that radiated from their pink, freckled faces. They acted as if I did not exist. Secure in themselves and familiar with each other and with all of the school's procedures, they ran past me, avoiding my eyes except to tease. One morning I found a crude drawing of myself that had been placed inside my desk. The figure had excessively curly hair and pierced ears, and was foolishly dressed in clothes that were much too big. Its feet were almost the size of the figure itself. The prankster had included a series of nonsensical syllables which seemed to come out of the caricature's mouth. The heading on the drawing was "The Spic." I studied it for a long while, tore it into a thousand pieces, and flushed it down the toilet at school.

That Friday on my way home, I noticed that some of the boys in my class were following me at a short distance. I continued to walk, clutching my books to my chest and glancing occasionally in their direction. There were six of them. I began to walk faster, realizing that they had also

97

accelerated their pace. They began to shout, "Hey, spic! hey, spic!" over and over again. Frightened, I threw down my books and ran as fast as I could across an empty lot. I was two blocks from home. Suddenly it seemed as if they were coming at me from every direction. They encircled me, preventing me from going another step, and began to shove me back and forth between them, lifting my skirt and shouting things that terrified me even though I couldn't understand their meaning.

One of them unzipped the zipper of his pants and began to play with his penis with his hand. Crying, I begged them in Spanish to let me go. The boy who seemed to be their leader shoved me so hard that I ended up on the ground. Covering my face with my hands, I continued to whimper.

They went around the circle they had formed, taking turns kicking me on the head, stomach, and back. Suddenly we heard a man's voice, clear and authoritative. He seemed to be shouting at the boys to stop. They stopped and looked up in the man's direction. One of them gave me a final kick in the leg, and they all ran away, leaving me lying there in the vacant lot.

I was almost in shock, and my forehead was bleeding quite a bit. The man approached me. He spoke softly, soothingly to me and gently helped me to my feet. I ran from him in the direction of the Marlin. Fortunately, Mami was not in the room when I arrived. Assuming that she had been delayed while cleaning the hotel, I took a shower and hid my torn dress. I looked at myself in the bathroom mirror for what seemed like hours. The small of my back hurt intensely, and my leg was beginning to swell. I forced myself to stop crying and began to speak firmly to my reflection in the mirror.

"You're going to show all those bastards!" I said. "You're going to learn perfect English. Every inflection, every word

98

is going to be as perfect as it can possibly be. You're going to show those bastards that you're every bit as good as they are, and better."

I heard the door of our room open and close, came out of the bathroom, and saw Mami set a bag of groceries on the bed. I approached her with a smile, knowing just what I was going to say.

"Look what happened to this clumsy daughter of yours." I showed her my leg and the bruises on my face.

Mami ran towards me with a puzzled look on her face.

"*Que pasó, Marcia?*" she said with concern, inspecting the cut on my cheek.

"I fell down the stairs at school," I said matter-of-factly.

She smiled herself, relieved by the knowledge that my bruises had only been caused by a fall.

"You must be more careful," she said. "Sometimes I wonder what was the point of spending all that money in Havana on dance classes. They're supposed to make a girl graceful, no?"

That Saturday afternoon I sat Mami down on the bed and explained to her the futility of my attending regular classes. I told her how painful it was for me to sit there all day not being able to comprehend one word that was spoken. I wanted to know if we could ask our caseworker for the names of some schools that might be better suited for an oddball like me. She willingly agreed, having sensed my unhappiness with the situation at the Riverside School. I refused to accompany her to the school on the following Monday when she went to withdraw me. Luckily, she did not insist that I go. I never set foot in the Riverside Junior High School again.

Our caseworker suggested that I attend the Woodrow Wilson School in the southwest section of the city. There were many Cuban children enrolled in the school, she said.

I was ecstatic. I would finally meet other kids like myself. I enrolled and was placed in a classroom consisting mainly of Cuban children, the exceptions being a few recent arrivals from Central and South America—children as bewildered as myself.

The teacher was bilingual. We were placed according to our level of proficiency in English. There were children of all ages in the class, the oldest being seventeen. I was assigned to the level I group. Slowly, we began to learn the language. We used baby books in order to learn. Dr. Seuss was more instrumental in my learning English than any formal text-book ever was. At fourteen I began to make sentences like a two-year-old.

"John is a boy. Mary is a girl. See the boy run."

I was still anxious about attending school. Although I felt more at ease at Woodrow Wilson, the toughness of the kids I went to school with frightened me. It was so different from the placid life at the Mother of Jesus School! Fights were always breaking out. Many of my classmates made love in the bathroom during recess. I'd sit in the john and hear them doing it in the adjoining stalls. The moment the bell rang at the end of the school day, I'd gather up my books and dash home. I never took the same route twice.

With my increased mastery of the language came the opportunity to be gradually introduced to courses conducted purely in English. Along with a few others of my Spanish classmates, I began to be taken by bus a few days a week to the Rickenbacker School in South Miami. It took us almost ninety minutes to get to school in the mornings. There, they established a classroom where all of us could continue our elementary English lessons. At the same time, however, we now had the opportunity to audit some classes in English. Eventually we began to participate in these classes. But most of the time we still remained isolated from the activities at Rickenbacker. We ate lunch as a separate group and forever watched the Yankees longingly. We wished that we could also participate in those very American school activities that took place around us. Cheerleading and spelling bees were my secret dreams.

All during this period, Mami and I longed to be reunited with Dad. His letters were few and came infrequently. Apparently censors inspected all the mail entering or leaving the island. Dad's letters arrived half-open, whole paragraphs scratched out in heavy black ink. We always wondered what harmless statements written by my father had been deleted. It was frustrating and depressing to have our relationship with him violated by these nameless, faceless intruders that omnipotently dictated what a person could express to a relative. Sometimes we'd send Dad individual pieces of gum and razor blades taped to the insides of our letters. As Cuba and the United States had broken diplomatic relations, anything made in America that reached Cuba without being confiscated was cherished by those still there. Since all letters had to travel via countries friendly with Cuba, letters sometimes took two months to arrive. A letter written in Cuba sometimes still comes through a country such as Mexico. Most never reach their destination.

To a Cuban, being related by blood implies a most sacred covenant. We feel the highest sense of responsibility to care for our own. Cubans living in America usually help support family members still in Cuba by covertly exchanging dollars for pesos or vice versa. Periodically, persons in the United States arrange for certain sums of pesos to be delivered to their relatives in Cuba. In order to do so, they pay a predetermined number of dollars to someone in America in need of American money. Once that payment has been made, a contact arranges for a corresponding amount in pesos to be delivered to someone on the island.

Arrangements are for the most part made by mail. This presents a problem since the transactions are illegal. Since mail is so carefully scrutinized, families resort to sending coded messages fraught with innuendos. The ratio of dollars to pesos is determined by demand. At times we have bought at the price of three pesos per dollar. At other times, we have paid as much as fifteen pesos per dollar.

We once wrote a letter to my father which said, "We are thinking of renting a small apartment. The only problem is that its only closet measures two feet by ten feet." In our letter we elaborated a bit on the pros and cons of the fictitious apartment. My father, having received the letter and understanding its meaning, promptly replied, "The apartment sounds very nice. I wouldn't worry about too small a closet. It sounds all right to me."

Having been given his okay as to the going rate, we notified the gentleman with whom we were to work out the details of the exchange.

Once in a televised speech, Castro joked about the gusanos and their implausible codes. Sarcastically he referred to someone who wrote a letter to Cuba about buying a bottle of prescription pills with only twenty inside. Following the broadcast, mail seemed to arrive even more infrequently.

In another letter to Dad, we wrote, "Nico's mother, Marta, poor woman, is all alone in Cuba. Be sure to go by and see her on her birthday, which is on the sixth. She is living now at_____." We went on to give him the woman's address.

Upon receipt of our letter, Dad went to see the woman. Introducing himself by only his first name, he said to her, "Your son Nico sends me. I have something for you." He proceeded to produce a long white envelope with 6,000 pesos. She accepted the envelope without saying a word.

They shook hands and he left. A check for $1,000 had already been cabled to us from New York by the woman's son.

Frequently, the people involved in a monetary transaction such as this are introduced by a mutual friend. Often, they have had no contact prior to the meeting at which they decide on a just ratio of trade. Rarely are there follow-up rendezvous unless there has been a mix-up in communication. Certain families become regular customers, regularly receiving vast sums of money from someone they have never met.

People in Cuba, fearing that all their savings would be confiscated, began to flock to the banks in order to withdraw their funds. While delivering a speech, Castro one day offhandedly commented on the futility of hoarding money at home.

"I have decided to change the color of our currency," he said. Che Guevara had been made president of Cuba's National Bank, and his signature would now appear on the bills. Castro also went on to warn the people that anyone found at home with large amounts of money would be imprisoned.

By now some people had amassed enormous sums at home. We know a man who had torn down parts of his bedroom wall and hidden about 3 million pesos within it. Since he was supposedly renovating his house, he was temporarily immune from the regular searches. His money, however, became worthless pieces of paper because of the new law.

The government established a policy whereby one could exchange up to 10,000 pesos. The money could not be withdrawn from a bank all at the same time. Dad himself had hidden a few thousand dollars of his savings at home. When this law was passed, he quietly distributed everything above the allotted 10,000 to friends and neighbors in 1,000-peso blocks. We found out about this when we were finally reunited with Dad.

The day following Castro's announcement about the currency changeover was chaotic. Families lined up for hours before dawn at the front doors of all the banks. People brought suitcases filled with the now worthless currency in order to exchange it for the new. Even if a person delivered 50,000 pesos to the teller, he was given only 10,000 in return. Millions lost their life savings on that day, Dad included.

Once while visiting Aunt Ramona, we met a man named Jose. He worked with Bill at his gas station and had been in the cigar manufacturing business in Havana. He had left the island with his daughter while his wife remained in Cuba caring for her sick mother. They had assumed that in a few months they'd be together again. Unfortunately, his wife's papers didn't clear immigration. It had been almost a year since his escape, and she was in desperate need of money.

During the course of the conversation, Mom suggested that it might be possible to arrange an exchange. For a certain number of dollars, she was sure Dad could deliver a sum of pesos to this man's wife. Jose was delighted and proposed that we call Dad right away in order to arrange an exchange. Jose was willing to write us a check for $500 that very night.

We spent the greater part of the evening trying to get through to Cuba by telephone. We finally reached Dad at around one o'clock in the morning. At the end of the conversation, Mom said that she had a favor to ask him. "We got a visit from Jose, your friend that was in the cigar business. Will you deliver the 2,000 cigars we are keeping for him in the garage to his wife Rona?" she asked.

Dad replied that he had forgotten where she lived.

"Take the boxes to her beauty parlor on _____," and she

104

gave him the woman's address. Dad said that he'd be glad to get rid of all those boxes as they were taking up a lot of space. He sent Jose his regards.

Mother told him that we loved and missed him, and that Jose had been very good to us.

"He has helped us out in every way he could. He has almost been too good," she said.

Once we hung up, the gentleman produced his checkbook and wrote us a check for $500. He bid us good-bye and good luck and, patting me on the head, left Ramona's.

We were later to learn that Dad had shown up at the woman's beauty parlor and had asked to see the owner. Dad's first words were that Jose had sent him. After ascertaining that the woman was indeed married to a man named Jose, Dad proceeded to hand her 2,000 pesos in cash. The woman was so grateful, she insisted that he stay awhile and have a cup of coffee with her. Dad told us how much he enjoyed being the only man in a beauty parlor and getting a glimpse of just what went on in such a place. He added that it had certainly been the most expensive cup of coffee he had ever had.

The outcome of a large number of attempted currency exchanges was not so successful.

The father of Sara, a good friend of mine in Cuba, is still serving time in a Cuban prison for attempting to trade pesos for dollars. Sara and her mother are in Miami. For Sara's mother, it has not been easy to live with the realization that their well-being was directly responsible for her husband's imprisonment. She was a newspaperwoman in Havana. Now she washes dishes at the lunch counter of Walgreen's Drug Store on Flagler Street. Fluency and eloquence in Spanish don't help her earn a living in an English-speaking country. Here, her skills are worse than useless. "What other type of work can I realistically obtain?" she asks.

One day Mami decided to try to get a better job so that we might have more money to live on. She asked me to let her borrow the Spanish-English dictionary that I used diligently at school. Together we scanned the *Miami Herald* employment section every day, looking up words in the job descriptions which we did not know. Her job working as a maid did not quite cover our living expenses. She told me that she was reluctant to go on welfare because it would be too painful and demoralizing for her. I knew how difficult it was for her just to visit the refugee center. She told me once that she'd rather starve than go there and beg. I wanted her to go. I only wanted better clothes than the ones I had to wear to school.

I did not quite understand her reservations, her pride. The families of most of my classmates at Woodrow Wilson were regularly receiving government checks. They dressed better than I did, and some of them actually owned television sets.

We continued to look in the paper for a suitable position for her. The job market was tight, and the selection was limited; it's not easy to find a job that doesn't require talking. For a while we tried without success to get her a factory job. I'd call the number listed in the newspaper for her. In my broken English, pretending to be Mom, I'd inquire about the positions available.

Attending regular classes in English was helping me tremendously. I could sense the fog that had engulfed me lifting. I'd overhear conversations on the bus and would actually understand some of the words that were being spoken. That was a breakthrough.

I became a permanent fixture at the Miami Public Library. All the employees there got to know me by my first name. I forced myself to read voraciously. There was nothing I couldn't tackle with the aid of my worn-out, faithful dictionary. Picture books with written captions were particularly helpful. In less than six months my effort was paying off; I was beginning to understand what was said to me and also able to make myself understood. I still had to articulate some of my thoughts with gestures, but I had made a start and could be Mom's translator when we went to the grocery store. Mami's progress with English was not so rapid.

I now realize how much easier it is for kids to adjust to a new environment and particularly to learn a foreign language. Mom tried evening classes for adults—English-as-a-second-language classes, they are now euphemistically called. After a while, Mami got discouraged and quit. Her heart just wasn't in it. She wasn't adjusting as well as I was. She did not want to adjust. All she wanted was to go back to Cuba—not today's Cuba, but the Cuba that her memories kept alive. She also missed Dad terribly. I'd find her reading his old letters in the middle of the night.

Getting Mom a factory job was not working at all. I could only do so much over the telephone. Once an interview had been arranged, she had to show up without me, her interpreter, to assist her. Inevitably, her limited knowledge of the language resulted in her not getting the job. To help, I'd write down potential interview questions and answers for her, and we'd rehearse them. I'd spell the words using the Spanish prounciation. *Employment* would become *emploiment, i* was *ai, job* was *yob.*

I was still uncertain about my own English and dreaded answering the telephone. It was harder for me to understand people when I could not see their faces. I'd bring myself to answer the phone in a voice deeper than my own, only to be told, "Mrs. Fuentes? I'm sorry but we need someone who speaks English a little better."

One day we saw an ad which specifically asked for a Spanish-speaking woman to act as a baby-sitter and to clean house. Excitedly, I called the woman.

"I own a chain of bowling alleys and I'm gone most nights. I need someone to take care of the house, watch over my three kids, and teach them a little Spanish," she said.

Right away I made an appointment for us to go out to her house.

"I have a daughter," I told her.

"Don't worry, Mrs. Fuentes, your daughter can stay with you, too. We have plenty of room." She sounded enthusiastic. We hastily packed our suitcase and left the Marlin. The manager was very kind. He told us that we could have our room back any time we wanted it.

Mrs. Corcoran's house was located in the Coconut Grove section of the city. She showed us around the house and introduced us to her children, three little blond tykes much younger than myself. It was decided that I'd do any translating that was required and that Mami would speak to the children only in Spanish.

"I'm divorced, and my new boyfriend is from Puerto Rico," she said.

She was an attractive woman in her mid-thirties. Even though it was early afternoon, she was already nursing a highball. The record player was blaring Latin tunes. Mrs. Corcoran asked my mother if she wanted a drink. Mami declined.

We were shown the bedroom we were to call home. It was in the back of the house and it faced the pool. I had not been in such spacious surroundings since Cuba. I was eager for Mami to accept the job.

"I'll give you both your room and board plus $50 a week," she said.

We felt good about the salary and liked Mrs. Corcoran's children. We looked forward to living there and moved in that very night. It seemed as if the house had not been cleaned for months. Dust gathered in the corners, and the refrigerator gave off a stench of rotting food. There was no milk in the refrigerator, only beer and wine.

Mrs. Corcoran did not return home for two days. Meanwhile, the children were totally unmanageable. They went around the house breaking their mother's ornaments and mischievously awaiting our reaction. During our third day there, they hit upon a game they insistently pursued. They'd chase Mom around the house with their toy bows and arrows, while laughingly imitating her speech. One of the little boys persisted in urinating on the couch, much to Mami's chagrin. They'd hide from us and force us to look for them all over the neighborhood. They were as incorrigible as they were adorable.

One night there was a loud knock at the door. A tall, heavyset man introducing himself as Mr. Corcoran let himself into the living room and sat down. The children were already in bed.

He waited for hours until Mrs. Corcoran and her boyfriend Ricky finally arrived, boisterous and drunk. The three of them got into a terrible fight. Both men began to hit each other. Mrs. Corcoran pounded with her fists on Mr. Corcoran. He slapped her so hard that her lips began to bleed. Ricky vacillated between trying to strike Mr. Corcoran and trying to get away from him.

Quietly, Mami and I went into our room and packed our few belongings. We wanted to get to Ramona's but didn't know how. We rode the Miami buses all night, finally arriving at Ramona's almost at dawn.

We set about the difficult task of finding Mother another job. Same tactics, same replies. She finally got a job through the paper as a companion to an elderly Cuban woman. The woman's family had been extremely wealthy in Cuba and had managed to put the bulk of their money in Swiss banks. The old woman was heartless and tyrannical. Every day she'd make Mom polish the soles of all her shoes. An insomniac, she'd wake up Mother in the middle of the night and make her give her a bath. Having Mother sponge her wrinkled body soothed the woman. She was always insulting us. She said all kinds of things to Mami once and made her cry. Mami retaliated by going into the old woman's closet and repeatedly spitting all over her clothes and shoes.

It had been over a year since we had seen Dad. Mom called him frantically and told him that if he didn't find a way to come and join us, we'd both be returning to Cuba no matter what. She was so fed up that day she didn't even care if the G2 overheard our conversation with him.

Dad told us that he'd see what he could do. Less than two months later we were reunited with him.

6

MY FATHER'S "ESCAPE" CAN-
not really be labeled as such. He signed over all that he had
honestly worked for, all of his life. In exchange he got the
appropriate exit papers. Then he bought his way aboard
one of the flights still making the daily trip from Cuba to
the United States.

The regime did not really care whether he remained or
not. Why should they? His holdings were infinitely more
valuable than he was. The government was reluctant to let
people between the ages of fifteen and twenty-seven leave
because the young were needed to work long hours at im-
plementing Fidel Castro's schemes. The government also
made it very difficult for doctors to get out. Their mass
exodus had left most hospitals understaffed. But Dad was
neither a young man nor a doctor. He wasn't very important. After all the time we had spent apart, he was finally
joining us in America.

Ramona lent Mami some money, and we rented a modest
one-bedroom apartment on 8th Street, the heart of "Little
Havana," the Cuban ghetto. It was unfurnished, so we slept
on the cots which Ramona lent us. We built a dining room
table from discarded orange crates and decorated the walls
with glossy pictures out of old magazines. Our home looked
beautiful to us once it was completed.

Ramona drove us to the airport to meet Dad. We hadn't seen him in over a year. When he stepped off the plane, he seemed smaller and thinner than I'd remembered him, but his face was still lit with that radiant, transforming smile. Our first encounter was awkward—we had been apart much too long. We all simply held onto each other and cried, relief and joy mixed up together with our fear.

Dad's arrival marked a turning point for us all. The finality of our move became more evident. We were three aliens, instead of just two. We were together, but we were strangers to all that surrounded us, longing for the familiar, for some structure that would give us security and a feeling of permanence. I sensed my father's dismay and disorientation. We would have to build a new life together from scratch.

When we got back to the apartment, Dad wanted to take a shower and freshen up, so Mami handed him an old mended towel with "The Marlin" inscribed on it. He held it in front of him and smiled sadly.

After his shower, we sat on one of the cots and tried to catch up on a year of news. I could see that he was anxious for Ramona to leave. He obviously wanted to say something meant only for us. Ramona stayed long enough to have some coffee with us and to display for Dad her rather limited repertoire of English words. She could fool me no more. Her disorientation, although veiled, was just as great as ours. It takes more than a few years for someone to feel truly comfortable in so new an environment. Immigrants are like plants torn up by their roots; many can't take the trauma and slowly wither away. The few luckier ones, those with a greater capacity for regeneration, survive the shock somehow and with time grow strong again. It is a simple question of survival.

Once Ramona left, Dad said that he had something to tell us.

"I was lucky to get out. They give people only twenty-four hours' notification. You never know when the official call is going to come, so you sit by the telephone, agonizing while you wait. You feel helpless, at the mercy of people you've never met. Your life is in their hands," he said.

I asked him what happens when you are forced to leave the house momentarily and they call.

"You miss your turn and have to start all over again. That's what happened to Afredo; it's now been almost two years since he first asked permission to leave," he said matter-of-factly.

He produced an American dime from his pocket.

"This is all that I was legally allowed to take with me. They give it to you so that you can make a telephone call once you arrive in the United States. They even confiscated at the airport the little gold medal my mother gave me before she died. My neck feels so bare without it."

He was fifty years old, didn't know any English, and all that he'd been able to bring with him was a dime and a change of shirt. I had never felt sorrier for him or for myself.

"It's going to be a momentous occasion every time I go to the bathroom for the next couple of days," he said with a sly grin.

The meaning of his words escaped us.

"I went to Dr. Jimenez's house last night. You know he's a confirmed gusano," he said.

We nodded.

"We hit on an ingenious plan several months ago while playing poker. To carry it out, I bought several truly magnificent diamonds on the black market. Last night Jimenez put them in some gelatin capsules for me, and toasting him with some wine, I swallowed them all."

His grin was triumphant.

"Aren't they going to tear your insides to shreds?" Mami was concerned.

"We don't think so. Jimenez gave me a lot of bicarbonate of soda as an antacid. The gastric juices shouldn't eat through the gems. Once they're out, we can sell them and get ourselves some real furniture for this place." He looked around the room with satisfaction.

The next few days were as bizarre as they were humorous. Whenever Dad felt the slightest need to defecate, the most minimal stirrings in his gut, he'd get his large aluminum bucket, bought specifically for the purpose, and patiently sit on it in the bathroom.

Once he'd moved his bowels, he'd bring out the pail and spread its contents on the newspapers Mami had laid out on the living room floor. Wearing rubber gloves, we'd take turns methodically going through the feces. The capsules had disintegrated completely, but the diamonds shone incongruously amid the excrement. They were intact. Every time we found one, we'd hug each other and laugh.

The juxtaposition of excrement and gems jolts the mind.

Swallowing the diamonds didn't even give Dad a stomachache. Mami gave him a laxative to speed up the process. They were all expelled in less than two days. We sold them all but one for whatever we could get. The last one we set in white gold and made into a ring. My parents gave it to me on my eighteenth birthday. It is my most treasured piece of jewelry —a stone that is symbolic of our odyssey. I intend to pass it on to my own daughter, in memory of Dad's cunning and courage. No amount of money in the world could ever make me part with it.

As the days went by, the full story of Dad's last year in Cuba emerged. While Dad diligently worked on making our new home as comfortable as he could, he told us amazing tales filled with sorrows.

"Juan Martinez hit upon a brilliant idea," he said. "He was afraid to keep the few pieces of jewelry he and his wife

114

owned in the house in case the G2 found them during one of their raids. He started a collection among his friends he was certain were gusanos. We itemized the pieces, putting them in separate boxes coded by number. Fernando Vasques, the mortician on Avenida de las Flores, hid all the valuables in an empty casket. About a month ago, we had a mock funeral at the cemetery in the Vedado for them. We even wore black! It was a beautiful ceremony. The burial went off without a hitch. According to the authorities, a Jose Perez is buried in that grave. A common enough name for uncommon stuff." He laughed, amused at his own and his friends' ingenuity.

"I don't think we'll live to go and collect," he told my mother. "We'll write down all the information for Marcia. Maybe if she ever gets to go back to Cuba, she can go on a treasure hunt of sorts."

I remained silent as he told this story. It all seemed so morbid to me. The thought of venturing at night into a cemetery, finding the grave of the fictitious Jose Perez, and digging up the contents of a tomb sickened me. What if we dug up the wrong Jose?

Dad went on to tell us the main reason he decided it was indeed time for him to leave the country.

He'd been lending his car to a friend in order that arms could be transported to isolated groups of gusanos that worked together for the purpose of overthrowing the regime. His friend had been caught while transporting some ammunition to Camaguey Province and was jailed. He was brutally interrogated at G2 headquarters on the Quinta Avenida so that he would reveal the names of those working with him. Dad would go by the headquarters every day and see his car parked in the lot. It was just a matter of time until its ownership was traced. The penalty for an act such as he had committed was twenty years' imprisonment.

His friend managed to send him a message which said, "Leave the island. I can't hold on much longer."

This man, Miguel, was the head of the counterrevolutionary movement. Dad said that his own increased involvement in the movement was placing him in more and more danger every day. It was a question of escaping or staying and fighting to make his country a democracy again. Could he risk never seeing his family again?

"It is a losing battle," he said, sighing. "They take the young and put dangerous ideas in their heads. Family doesn't count anymore. Friends don't matter. Older people are afraid, and with good reason. Our country has almost doubled in population since the revolution. It's fun for the young to be given guns and told they are the guardians of the revolution. They are made to feel important and provided with encouragement by the government to disagree with their parents. The children whose minds are being poisoned, they're the ones who will carry on the revolution. It's a losing battle," he repeated. "That's what made me finally decide to leave."

I remember asking him what had happened to Miguel.

"That story has a happy ending, Marcia. Three individuals impersonating high officials in Castro's army showed up at the G2 with a phony authorization of release supposedly signed by the chief of the Cabana prison. They showed it to the guard on duty and demanded that they be taken to the prisoner's cell. Approaching Miguel, who apparently didn't let on that he recognized the men, they began to beat him up in front of the guard saying that he was a son of a bitch, and that they were going to fix him. They thanked the guard on duty and dragged Miguel out to their car, speeding away.

"One of the men who rescued Miguel is still in charge of the Committee for the Defense of the Revolution in his

116

neighborhood. The gusanos know that he is on their side and use his services whenever they can. The man's rationale for his unorthodox position is that he can be of more help from within than otherwise."

During those early days in Miami, I took Dad on walks around the neighborhood so that he'd become familiar with what had now become a part of me. I showed him my school, the church we attended every week, and the grocery store where we did our shopping. The store was in a dilapidated building two blocks from our apartment. It was called the Liborio. The term *Liborio* symbolizes to Cubans what Uncle Sam means to Americans. Liborio's caricature is always a little guy with a large straw hat, smoking a thick cigar. Many businesses in Miami have Liborio for their logo so that they will be quickly identifiable as Cuban-owned. Such a logo is also a public statement of the store owner's patriotism. You may live far away from Cuba, but Liborio is always in your heart.

We were already living in Miami during the missile crisis. Cubans in our neighborhood gathered at our house to talk politics and exchange reactions to the crisis. Most of the people there felt that the publicity being given to the incident was a tactical ploy to make the administration in Washington look good. "They want everybody to forget about the Bay of Pigs real fast," said one man. A few weeks later rumors began to arrive from those still on the island. According to the people still in Cuba, there had been no actual site inspection of the missiles supposedly being withdrawn from the island. People acknowledged that some had been withdrawn, but they suspected that the bulk of them remained. It was also rumored that what looked like missiles to the Americans from the air were Royal Palm trees from Oriente Province covered with canvas and made to look like missiles from a distance. Those still in Cuba today are convinced that many missiles remain. Some people living in Oriente say that they have actually seen them being transported underground.

To learn English, Dad enrolled in a class at a local community college. He looked up old friends from home and adapted marvelously to the frustration of daily searching for a job. It seemed as if he always carried the classified section of the *Miami Herald* under his arm. His optimism knew no bounds, even though he was constantly being turned down either because of his age or because of his inability to speak English. I had personally been through all that while Mom and I were living alone. But now we were together. What did it matter that we were terribly poor? We had each other. As far as we were concerned, we lived in the freest country in the world and had an unshakable faith in ourselves and in the future.

We agonized, however, about our depleting cash reserves. The funds from the sale of the diamonds were quickly being exhausted, and we were worried sick about what would happen to us once all the money was gone. It got so bad that we had nineteen dollars in cash left to our name.

I remember watching Dad empty his pockets on the dining room table with Mami immediately following his example—a ten-dollar bill, a crisp five, four singles and a bit of loose change. Not much at all, I thought, focusing intently on their solemn faces. The day before, I had seen a particularly beautiful doll in the window of Lydia's Drugstore. It didn't matter that I was too old for dolls. I wanted her, to replace one that I had left behind. I now painfully realized that my beautiful doll was well beyond my reach. How selfish and unrealistic of me, I thought to myself. How much had I taken for granted before!

I missed my family of dolls, particularly Carmela, the

one with the magnificent chiseled face and red, puckered lips. Papi had made me a cloth replica of her which he had painstakingly stuffed with old kitchen rags. Mami had sewn long tresses onto the doll's cloth head, using strands of golden yarn which she had meticulously arranged to cover its whole scalp. Mami had even made a blue dress for my new doll, identical with the one Carmela used to wear. "She's not the same," I nevertheless cried to myself at night. "She's not my old Carmela." I worried about leaving Carmela behind and could not forgive myself for having deserted her. I wondered in the darkness if the little girl who now owned her gave Carmela the attention that she required. Did she take the time to wash her dress every week, as I had done? I knew how particular Carmela was about keeping herself immaculately clean. Feeling very sorry for myself and for Carmela, I would bury my face in the pillow and cry myself to sleep.

Mr. Prieta from next door had suggested to Papi that he go and apply at a downtown hotel that was hiring. Excitedly, he put on his one suit, bought especially for the occasion, and left for an interview. We didn't know what kind of work it would be, but somehow didn't care. Getting a job, any job, was what mattered. His salary, the nature of the work itself, and the hours were but insignificant details, immaterial bits of information. "As long as it's legal," Papi had wishfully said.

Miami was brimming with Cubans. Hordes of refugees arrived daily. Homeless, jobless, and bewildered, they assembled outside Miami's employment agencies. People waited at dawn in front of the *Miami Herald*'s building for the classifieds to roll from the presses. I usually saw the crowds forming outside the building on my way to school. I tended to walk quickly past the people, purposefully avoiding the optimism reflected in their faces. Thinking this early morning effort gave them an edge over the many others who now looked in vain for work, they spoke animatedly to each other. Many held thermoses of strong, hot coffee tightly under their arms.

For months Dad had tried both the classifieds and the employment agencies, to no avail. Nevertheless, that night he stormed into the house as Mami was cooking dinner. "I have a job!" he shouted, grabbing Mami by her waist and whirling her about the room. Out of breath, he soon dropped himself onto the couch and beckoned me to sit on his lap.

"You are looking at a working man," he said beaming, the wrinkles around his eyes creasing deeply.

Papi became a bellboy at the Star Hotel in downtown Miami. Luckily, the job did not really require much English, so he could get on primarily by gestures. There wasn't much activity at that time of night anyway, just a few drunks to deal with and a couple of aging call girls who got to know Papi by name and were no problem. At home he'd sleep part of the day and faithfully study his English lessons in the afternoons. Mami worried that he was pushing himself too hard with work and school, plus a part-time job at a nearby gas station. He really looked tired and gaunt. It was also a difficult adjustment for all of us to have Papi's time schedule reversed. We'd try to tiptoe around the house so as not to awaken him. The curtains drawn, we moved about in semi-darkness, fiercely mindful of Papi and his sleep. It was always nighttime inside our house, yet we did not mind. We guarded Papi's few rest hours as loyally as two watchdogs.

Dad usually arrived home at around six o'clock in the morning. I'd try to be awake for him so that we could have a little time to chat before I went off to school. He'd then sleep until around two in the afternoon, when Mami usually awakened him for lunch.

Afterwards, he'd sit at the table and study his lessons. We'd daily compare notes on what each of us was learning, amused at the similarities we encountered in our respective homework assignments. His motivation to learn the language was awesome. I'd sit on the kitchen step, away from his immediate line of vision, and watch him study. I'd hear him repeating his vocabulary words over and over again, as he attempted to perfect his pronunciation. His notebooks, thorough and up-to-date, made me feel guilty yet nevertheless forced me to work harder. Sometimes we would carry on awkward little conversations in English in order to practice. Somewhat embarrassed by our heavy accents, we avoided each other's eyes as we softly uttered the unfamiliar words. Papi often fell asleep in the afternoons while studying. I'd watch his hands relax, gradually releasing their grip on his notebook. His thick glasses invariably slid down his nose as he'd slump slightly forward, his breathing becoming deeper and more regular.

I'd scrutinize him for hours, finding comfort in the reassuring tempo of his snores. He had repeatedly told me to wake him up immediately if he ever fell asleep during lesson time, but I'd ignore his instructions and opt for letting him sleep as I looked on. After his lessons he'd go over to Heraldo's gas station for a while before his regular job began. Sometimes, on the weekend, we'd take a bus over to Miami Beach, where we'd walk endlessly on the sand along Ocean Avenue, watching the sea and feeding bread crumbs to the sea gulls. "The land at the other side of this ocean, where these very waves touch shore, is our Cuba, Marcia," Papi often said, looking with longing toward the horizon.

Breathing in the salty air and feeling the mist and the sun on our faces reminded us inevitably of home. We could close our eyes and recall exactly what it felt like to sit on our beloved porch. We often sat for hours on the wooden park benches, imagining ourselves to be back home.

Throughout this period, we felt as if a part of us was missing, as if a limb or an eye had been mercilessly torn from us. All that we could call our own lay ninety miles away, close in distance, but forever unreachable. Our lives had been so dramatically affected that, in desperation, we fiercely clung to the few familiar fragments that remained. We maintained a bond, however fragile, with what had been, inadequately attempting to re-create a reality that was no more.

During these early days in Miami, an invisible umbilical cord tightly linked us to the past. We shopped only in stores that were Cuban-owned, finding solace in transactions made in Spanish with other refugees like ourselves. Sometimes we rode over to Hialeah just to shop at a particular pharmacy that was owned by a Cuban family we had been friendly with in Cuba. "We have to help each other," Papi told me once, "even if it's sometimes a little bit inconvenient." A little directory began to circulate telling immigrants exactly which were Miami's Cuban establishments. These businesses usually carried the very names they'd used in Cuba and were thus easily identifiable. In such stores you were always sure that you would be treated with kindness and respect. Often, the owners offered you guava pastries and espresso and, amiably introducing themselves, shared with you the circumstances of their own escapes. At times, you encountered by chance friends who you thought were dead or in prison.

One morning the garbage man knocked at our door to collect the bill, only to be greeted by my parents with hugs and shouts of disbelief.

"Rolando, it's you! My god, I can't believe you made it out."

Inevitably, the specifics of his coming to America unfolded.

"And your wife, is she out?"

"No, it's been six years now. She was to stay behind just until her mother's health improved, but her visa was suddenly revoked, so she remains in Cuba," answered Rolando.

An old university friend of Dad's, Rolando had been a physician in Cuba. He knew so little English that garbage collecting had been the only job he was able to find while he learned the language. Somewhat embarrassed, he collected the money for the bill and walked away with downcast eyes. Encountering close friends from home was what really made Miami such a good place for Cubans to live. You never knew what ghosts from home you would come across walking down Flagler Street.

Adjusting to life in America was hardest for Mami. She spent her days alone at home and began to withdraw more and more into herself. At least Papi had his work and I had school. We were not allowed the opportunity to isolate ourselves from the world, as Mami so easily could, and did.

I wanted desperately to draw Mami out of her shell, to convert her once more into the sparkling person she had been. Coming home from school, I always ran exuberantly up the two flights of stairs to our apartment and let myself in. Every afternoon, I automatically drew back the curtains Mami still insisted on keeping shut, even when Papi began working the day shift.

"It will make you feel better, Mami," I used to say.

Sometimes, I pretended to want to go to the park, just so that I could get her out of the house. She usually refused to go, feigning a headache.

Late at night, I sometimes overheard my parents arguing bitterly.

"We now live in America, so let's make the best of it," Papi would say with annoyance.

I usually placed the pillow tightly over my ears, attempting to drown out the shouting. I was not accustomed to hearing Mami and Papi fight, and their anger and frustration filled me with dread. Papi usually relented once Mami began to shed a few tears. A part of him understood how very sad she was and how her sadness colored her attitude toward America. "Take a class, or a part-time job. Look up some old friends. I hear Isabel and Pancho have finally gotten out and are living in South Miami," Papi would say, well aware of the futility of his advice.

Mami got into the habit of daily playing a record of the Cuban national anthem she had come across at El Liborio. I clearly remember the album cover, nostalgically plastered with glimpses of Havana and of its tall, majestic palm trees.

Over and over the album played. It played so often that I grew to hate its melody. I was ecstatic the day it got scratched and had to be thrown away. But its loss made Mami despondent for days. For months, she never bothered to dress in the mornings. She would sit in the kitchen wearing her tattered print robe, thinking of Cuba and of the life we'd left behind.

"Let's go over to the beach and watch the ocean," Papi and I would suggest hopefully.

Mami would not bother to respond. She would just look through us with bloodshot eyes and that blank stare on her face I grew to dread.

With legal immigration channels permanently closed, those that still remained in Cuba were resorting to more and more audacious and dangerous alternatives in order to leave the country. My parents were often congratulated on our luck at having been successfully reunited in America. We were one of the few families that were still intact. Most of our acquaintances had been by now permanently separated from their loved ones.

Mami told us one evening at dinner that she wished to

124

help Berta, her best friend still in Cuba, get out. We listened intently, as we had not seen Mami so excited about anything in a long time.

While shopping at El Liborio, she had casually struck up a conversation with a Cuban fisherman named Alfredo. He boasted of the frequent trips he made to Cuba and assured Mami that he could bring somebody to America for $500. The fisherman gave Mami his word that he could get Berta safely out of Cuba and offered her his telephone number. She was to call whenever she had the money ready for him.

"That's a lot of money to us these days, Juana. You know that the little bit we've saved is to go for the purchase of a car," my father said quietly to her.

Mom was so insistent that Dad finally agreed to foot the bill for Berta's escape. She left the table and went immediately over to the telephone to call Alfredo. He instructed her to bring the specified amount, a photograph of herself, and Berta's address in Cuba to his house immediately. Dad had real reservations about Alfredo's honesty but at Mother's insistence decided to go ahead and pay the man.

Berta arrived in Miami less than a month later unharmed. A widow, she moved in with her married son and his wife in Little Havana. Her son had been overjoyed at the possibility that Alfredo could get her out of Cuba. Once they were reunited, he repaid us the full $500 for Berta's escape.

The week she arrived we had her over for dinner. According to Berta, Alfredo showed up at her house without warning one night. Showing her mother's picture, he asked to speak privately to her. She let him in.

"I have come to get you out of the country. Don't be afraid, I do it all the time. It's not really the money. Let's just say it's my personal way of contributing to the cause," he said.

Berta was told to stand on the corner of Manrique and

Concordia on the following evening at six o'clock, wearing a long-sleeved black blouse.

"It's certainly not giving me much time to get ready, but I'll be there," she said.

"Don't bring a suitcase, only a purse," he said before he left.

Berta was approached promptly at six by a sweating, nervous couple in their early forties who refused to identify themselves.

"We're leaving, too. Alfredo told us to pick up a woman fitting your description. You're Berta, aren't you?" said the man, looking around.

They drove for hours in silence to the bus station in Santa Clara. They spotted Alfredo inside the terminal. With a quick jerk of his head he signaled them to walk in the direction of the racks of magazines on the left side of the station.

Alfredo stood casually next to the three of them.

"Everything is fine. There are others here. They don't know each other, but they know me. We're waiting for our last passengers, a woman and her son," he said.

He walked away. Suddenly they saw a woman and a young boy of about sixteen entering the station. The woman appeared to be coaxing the boy to sit down. They watched him pacing nervously around the station, biting his nails. Suddenly, he began to scream.

"*Tengo miedo! tengo miedo!*" ("I am afraid!") he yelled again and again.

A militiaman approached the woman solicitously. Alfredo ran towards Berta and pretended to greet and hug her.

"Let's all meet here at the same time tomorrow. The group's got to disperse. Go to a movie or something," he whispered.

The couple decided to return to Havana that very night.

"I have a bad feeling about this whole mess," said the

126

woman apologetically. Berta checked into a rooming house under an assumed name. The following evening a group of seven people reassembled at the station and followed Alfredo out to the parking lot, where they were told to get into a dark blue van. The van took them along back roads to the coast, where they were to rendezvous with a fishing boat manned by Alfredo's brother. They waited in the dark for over an hour, huddled behind some rocks. Finally they heard a boat approaching and saw a light go on and off three times. They were picked up with no problem and arrived in Florida on the following day.

We never saw Alfredo again but read about him in the newspapers a few months later. Apparently he did make trips to Cuba regularly. He'd take arms and medicines into the country and always bring people out with him. The paper said that Hurricane Flora had demolished his small vessel. The Coast Guard found Alfredo and another man clinging to some loose boards a few miles off the Tampa coast. The boat had been full to capacity with men, women, and children. All others were dead. Carrying no identification whatsoever, they were taken to the Pan American Hospital. There, the reporters interviewed the men. We watched the interview on the ten o'clock news.

Alfredo, aware that his travels to Cuba were illegal, nevertheless acknowledged them.

"I will continue to make the trips to Cuba as long as there are people there longing for freedom," he said.

A few months later we learned that he'd been caught in Cuban waters and shot by a firing squad.

Several groups of men based in Miami regularly landed by boat on the island. Their main purpose was to carry arms and explosives to those people working against the government from inside the country. They also made contact with newly recruited gusanos, and trained them to handle explosives and carry out acts of sabotage. They often brought back to the United States gusanos whose lives, for whatever reason, were in danger. Many gusanos were brought to America for training and were then returned home. Some traveled regularly between Cuba and the United States.

Evelio Martinez made several clandestine trips a year to Cuba by boat. He was called The Chameleon by those in the Cuban underground. For every trip that he made to Cuba, he was provided with a set of false identification papers—a driver's license, a syndicate card, and a clinic card. He once went to Cuba and pretended to be a lottery ticket vendor for two weeks. He frequented the outskirts of an important plant he was later to bomb. He sold lottery tickets to both workers and management while learning the schedule and floor plans of the plant. Another time he masqueraded as a militiaman, complete with military identification card. When he told me about that particular operation, he said that he'd rather not go into details.

During the Bay of Pigs, Evelio was stranded on a small raft a few miles out of Cuban waters. He floated for days, certain that he'd soon be rescued. His compatriots sent out search parties to look for him. A small plane equipped with a metal detector found him still alive when he had all but given up hope. He carried a rifle with him which the metal detector picked up on its screen.

Mami had bought a powerful radio so that she could pick up stations in Cuba. Dad and I didn't enjoy having Mom glued to the radio every night, tormenting herself with government propaganda. But she insisted on listening to the programs. She even listened to Fidel. Fidel was on the radio one night, and we were preparing to sit through one of his usual lengthy speeches, when he announced something very interesting indeed.

128

"The gusanos say that people here are not free to leave the country if they choose to. Anyone who wishes to dock in Camarioca in Matanza Province and pick up a relative may do so," he said. The following morning, the Cuban colony in Miami was in an uproar. Cubans living in Mexico and Spain flew into Miami by the hundreds. Numerous signs could be seen posted outside the houses along 8th Street— "Boat to go to Cuba for sale" or "Boat wanted for going to Cuba."

Meanwhile, in Cuba, thousands made the trip to Camarioca on foot. People slept by the side of the road. They left all that they owned behind. All the telephone circuits to Cuba were busy for hours. We finally got hold of my Aunt Carmen in Havana. The news was hardly publicized in Cuba, so she had heard nothing about Camarioca.

"Go to Camarioca," we told her.

A makeshift government office was set up right on the beach. All types of vessels approached the beach. People yelled from the boats. "We're Cubans, we've come to pick up our family!" The exiles brought chickens and hams with them on their boats to use as bribes. The militia allowed the family of the highest bidder to embark first.

Many of the "government officials" charged with the task of filling out the appropriate forms for departure were near-illiterate campesinos drafted into the militia from their usual work in the sugar cane fields. A number of soon-to-be refugees could be seen helping the bewildered campesinos in charge decipher the numerous forms.

Manolo, Aunt Carmen's husband, had bought himself a gray Oldsmobile during the first year of the revolution. A neighbor of his, a colonel in the Army, periodically asked Manolo and Carmen to sell it to him. Cars had become extremely scarce by then. There were no parts to repair old models, and few new cars were being imported. Manolo al-

129

ways refused. They lived in Varadero and had even gotten into the habit of using public transportation for their trips to Havana, two hours away, in order to maintain the Oldsmobile in good condition.

Carmen's papers were in order, but not Manolo's. When the opportunity arose to leave Cuba by way of Camarioca, Manolo immediately made a visit to the Colonel's house.

"I'm ready to make you a deal concerning the car," said Manolo.

"So you've heard the news, gusano," answered the Colonel with a smile.

"Yes, can you do anything for me?"

"You willing to leave tomorrow?" was the reply.

When Manolo returned home he told Aunt Carmen the good news. My aunt began to cry.

"Manolo, Linda and Jorge have to come, too!"

Carmen wanted to get her sister and brother-in-law out of the country also.

"But Carmen, their papers are not in order either," said Manolo.

"Please, go and talk to the Colonel again," Carmen begged.

Manolo walked across the street and knocked on the man's door.

"Back so soon?"

"I've got to get two more people out with us, or Carmen won't go."

"What's going to happen to your house?"

"I guess that it'll be confiscated, like everyone else's."

"Transfer its ownership directly to me and you can take with you as many gusanos as you want."

This arrangement suited Manolo just fine. He figured that everything he had would be lost no matter what. He'd rather his old neighbor get it all than a stranger.

"Colonel, you've got yourself a deal."

130

The following morning seven of them in all were personally driven to Camarioca by the Colonel in his official government car. The group carried no money with them. Aunt Carmen was allowed to take with her four dresses, a pair of pajamas, and two pairs of shoes. She was forced to turn in all her jewelry, including an old watch that she had worn every day for years. They were put haphazardly aboard a yacht owned by a prominent American businessman who had volunteered his boat to help as many Cubans as possible escape. The man owned a chain of department stores in Florida and employed a large number of Cuban refugees. His generosity on that day cannot ever be repaid.

The area between Cuba and the Florida coast is called the Corredor de la Muerte, or Hell's Corridor. The name is appropriate because it is in those treacherous waters that the majority of those trying to escape from the island have drowned or been shot down. But my aunt and uncle and their friends crossed the Corredor de la Muerte in safety and relative luxury, arriving in Miami at dawn on the following day. You might have read about Aunt Carmen or seen her picture in the paper. She was one of the first immigrants to land. She carried a statue of Jesus of Nazareth in her arms, and when she disembarked, she fell to her knees crying and kissed the American soil beneath her feet.

As a result of the exodus from Camarioca, Cuban children arrived in Miami by the boatload, unaccompanied by their parents. They were temporarily taken to a special camp in Opa Locka, Florida, and eventually placed in foster homes. A friend of mine, Ana Ramirez, was such a child-immigrant. Her parents, unable to leave the island themselves, chose the painful option of sending their daughter to the States alone. She has lived since then with a series of foster families in Miami, both Cuban and American. As one of the thousands of Cuban "orphans" scattered throughout the country, Ana

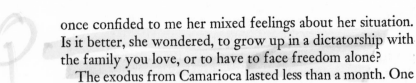

once confided to me her mixed feelings about her situation. Is it better, she wondered, to grow up in a dictatorship with the family you love, or to have to face freedom alone?

The exodus from Camarioca lasted less than a month. One morning, displeased with the large numbers of people flocking to Camarioca, Castro decreed that no more Cubans could leave the country in that manner.

Some people were still being arbitrarily allowed to embark on the numerous vessels still congregating on the bay. Others were not so lucky. Many families became permanently separated at Camarioca. Men and women were made to wait their turn in separate places, so many couples that had assumed they would be leaving together were never to see each other again.

When they got to Florida, the Camarioca refugees were each given an envelope containing fifty dollars by a Presbyterian association. They were served lunch, systematically interviewed by the authorities, and given a physical examination. The formalities usually lasted until about 3 A.M. on the morning following their arrival. Then they were finally allowed to leave the compound and join the relatives waiting for them.

Carmen and Manolo live in Miami these days. Manolo is a janitor in a factory that manufactures furniture. He was sixty and graying when he arrived. After being turned down for various jobs because of his age, he began to lie a little and dye his hair coal black. He feels that he is a lucky man to have obtained a job. After all, who in Florida needs an aging, Spanish-speaking lawyer with absolutely no knowledge of the American legal system?

132

7

I CONTINUED TO MAKE RAPID progress in school. Because I was young, it was much easier for me to pick up the language than it was for Mami and Papi. I felt increasingly comfortable with my new language and culture. I was so proud of my progress that I actually welcomed the opportunity to speak English. I started to volunteer fearlessly to act as the family's interpreter, and began to enjoy doing errands for my parents that required fluency in English. Acculturating myself quickly and completely became my all-consuming challenge.

I took on a series of part-time jobs in the afternoons and on Saturdays in order to help out at home. I remember lying about my age to obtain a position as salesgirl at Lydia's drugstore. I could see myself bypassing adolescence, becoming a little adult overwhelmed by numerous responsibilities and obligations. I was transformed into the only link between my parents and the outside world. I was their interpreter, their mentor—the means through which society channeled to them all kinds of crucial, logistical information. I was the clearing house that allowed us to survive, day by day, amid America's complexities.

"Lots of papers always need filling out, in America," Papi often complained, thoroughly disgusted and confused.

At my most optimistic moments, I saw myself as a bridge

between two cultures, in the privileged position of always having two alternative ways of looking at the world. Most of the time, however, I viewed myself as an outsider, as an unwanted guest.

I detected the antagonism which many Americans felt at having so many of us settle in Miami. I tried to excuse away their prejudice, realizing how threatening it must seem to have such a large influx of us make Miami our home. We violated every territorial instinct of the native-born by our mere presence. At times I even internalized their perceptions of us and saw myself as somewhat inferior because of my origins. At bus stops I stood back in deference, letting Americans walk ahead of me. For a long time it hurt me to have strangers I passed on the street avoid my eyes. It was only later that I learned this apparent unfriendliness was just one of the many small cultural differences between Cuba and the States which only the passage of time would reveal to me.

Most of my young Cuban friends were experiencing, as I was, a great deal of ambivalence about our Cuban heritage. It was puzzling and paradoxical to feel both pride and shame in what you were. I felt confused by the conflicting values and life-styles I witnessed about me.

My dearest friend, Marta, began to insist that I speak to her only in English and that I call her "Marty." Whenever we went to a movie with a group of refugees, she pretended not to know us and would sit alone in one of the back rows, cringing in the darkness whenever things got a little lively up front, where the rest of us were.

"You just talk too loud and make me feel embarrassed," she told me once, lowering her eyes in shame.

One evening we both went with a group of friends to hear a concert at school. Dad had been made manager at the Star and given a raise, so there was a little more money for such luxuries as tickets. Marty, as usual, opted for sitting on the opposite side of the auditorium. Carmen, a heavyset young girl who had also attended the Mother of Jesus School in Havana, was fed up with Marty's attitude. She yelled at her across the room in Spanish, her eyes ablaze. "Hey, Marta, you think you're too good for us?"

Marty bristled with annoyance. Torn between both points of view, I was at a loss as to whose side to take, whose position to defend.

"I only came along with you because I'm not allowed to date," Marty yelled back.

I could see her point. Dating was becoming an issue for all of us.

"Nice señoritas don't go out alone with boys," our families firmly told us. For our parents, it was disturbing to compare our country's stricter values with those embraced by the Americans. Fiercely clinging to the old ways, they upheld their Cuban customs, convinced that we would eventually see their point of view. Most of us grudgingly accepted the restrictions our families imposed, longing nevertheless for the freedom allowed our American counterparts. We wanted to date and wear high heels, to be real Americans. No one in Miami wanted to take out a girl who required a chaperone. We were different enough, without trying to live up to our parents' outmoded ideas about respectability—"when I was your age" compounded by "back in the old country."

I remember the humiliation I felt when I realized that Papi intended to escort me to my high school prom. For an instant, I seriously considered feigning a sudden illness, an acute attack of some obscure disease, that would prevent me from attending the event.

Only seeing Papi's humble bouquet dissuaded me from refusing to go.

"We'll have a real good time tonight at your school party, little girl," he said while handing me daisies, his gentle face lighting up in expectation. How could I tell Papi that I'd rather go alone than with him? How could I explain something that I myself did not fully understand? "In America, you look foolish if your Papi takes you to the prom," I phrased over and over again in my mind, lacking the courage to utter the words aloud.

I chose to attend the prom with Papi after all. Rising above some of my classmates' insensitive smirks, we managed to have a wonderful time. I realized on that crisp, cool Miami night that no matter what I did or how hard I tried, I would never be able to run away from what I was . . . and that I should not want to. Only by coming to terms with my heritage would I be genuinely freed to accept myself.

Yet, what was I really? A conglomeration of dichotomies and paradoxes—a Cuban-American collage, hyphen and all, awkwardly struggling for a comfortable niche somewhere between the diffused boundaries of the familiar and the unknown. At seventeen, I concluded that the trick was to swim with the current. I wanted consciously and objectively to choose the best of both worlds, incorporate it into my life-style. Yet, how difficult it is to achieve that tenuous balance and not lose a part of yourself in the process!

I felt a part of both worlds, yet fully a member of neither. Torn apart by two conflicting realities, I was unable to claim either one as wholly my own. It was only painfully, and very gradually, that my new identity gained in substance. With the passing of time my memories of Cuba began to dim, and the overwhelming desire to return slowly gave way to hopeful dreams concerning my new life in America.

I continued to live in Miami until I turned eighteen. I

was one of the lucky ones. Consciously, I did not allow myself to become discouraged either by my studies or by the agonizing prejudice those about me exhibited. By sheer persistence I eventually graduated from high school and was soon afterwards accepted by a prestigious women's college in Massachusetts.

I was so elated on the day the letter of acceptance finally arrived that I broke Mami's favorite vase while jumping up and down in the living room. I tightly clutched the yellow piece of paper against my breast in disbelief.

Mami and Papi were somewhat reluctant to have me go. Mami changed the subject whenever the topic of my impending departure came up.

"Why don't you stay here among your people and go to beauty school?" she hopefully suggested once while stroking my hair.

I tried to explain as best I could that I simply could not pass up this opportunity.

"This is my chance to really help all of us," I told them with conviction.

"But don't you want to stay here with us and meet a nice, young, Cuban man?" Mami persisted.

"Here in America, even if you're a woman, getting an education opens up a lot of possibilities, Mami."

I was adamant about accepting the college's offer. Mr. Jones, my guidance counselor at school, had helped me research whatever grant options were available to me. I was confused about the exact category I belonged in regarding my college funding. Mr. Jones and I agreed that I should check the box marked "minority." Yet we were both puzzled about another question. Was I, as a Cuban refugee, a "Latino," a "Spanish surnamed person," a "third world member," or "other"?

137

Mr. Jones patiently tried to explain how crucial this information was if I expected to be given the coveted scholarship. "Something about quotas," he said.

After submitting the scholarship application, I ran to the mailbox daily, always saying a small prayer as I opened it. I had already made up my mind to go, even before the issue of my scholarship was settled. I diligently set aside a portion of my summer earnings to buy myself a plane ticket and my first winter coat.

"No more charity from strangers," I said firmly to myself whenever I put some money aside.

The anticipated letter finally arrived. I had the scholarship, and would go to Massachusetts to school. My parents could not afford for both to fly up with me, so it was decided that Papi would accompany me, as his English was better.

When our plane landed at Kennedy Airport, I was struck by the cosmopolitan attitude of the people there. For the first time in a number of years, I did not feel stigmatized. The international quality of the city made allowances for people of all backgrounds to live side by side in harmony. I liked New York immediately.

My excitement grew during our drive north, toward the campus. How very pleasant people were to us! Strangers took the time to help us whenever we got lost along the way.

At the school, Papi spent the first two days of orientation with me, amazed at the turning leaves and the snow-capped mountains in the distance. To save money, we had decided to share a modest little room at a boarding house near the campus. I remember how uncomfortable our arrangement made the landlady feel.

"You going to learn to ski, Americana?" Papi asked me, his eyes twinkling. I knew that deep inside he approved of what I was doing. He had enough faith in me to know when to let go, and he realized that my wanting an education was a good thing.

We were both aware, when it was time for him to go, that I was on the threshold of yet another vastly different life. I felt exhilarated, yet very much afraid. Having managed to cross the abyss between two cultures, I was now up against the even tougher barrier of social class. Only through education would I propel myself into the mainstream of American life. The fashionable, self-assured girls with whom I would be living inhibited me. Everyone seemed so at home in her surroundings! Yet I looked forward to having a roommate at college and imagined our sharing in the discoveries that being university students would bring. While awaiting my room assignment, however, I learned that I was not to be assigned a roommate after all. Everyone seemed to have already paired off as I stood by, uncomfortably, in the periphery. The Dean of Students finally explained that I would occupy one of the single rooms on campus.

"You're quite a lucky girl," she told me, detecting my disappointment.

Apparently, it was the school's policy not to assign roommates to foreign students. I was hurt. Apparently, it was not enough that I already considered myself an American. As far as the school administration was concerned, I was still not quite one of them.

Perhaps they were right. After being shown to my room, I immediately began to make it livable by hanging my photographs of Cuba on the walls. I wanted to commit myself to my new life, yet derived a sense of comfort from the familiar images that looked down upon me from the bare, light-blue walls.

I soon realized that I was the only Cuban on campus. There were a few other Latin American students, however, whose stay in this country was to last only until the comple-

139

tion of their education. I really envied those Latins, with countries to which they could return. They looked a little like tourists, carrying their cameras with them to class.

As the only Cuban on campus, I did not know how people would react to me. My experiences in Miami had nourished my insecurity, yet I veiled my fears in a tight shield of bravado and looked optimistically ahead. Eventually I found out that I was actually the only Cuban in town. Nevertheless, as the townspeople held no strong, preconceived notions about us, they basically accepted me at face value as just another student. Their interest in me did not go beyond mere intellectual curiosity, and I was grateful. I did not want my background to precede me anymore, to allow people to stereotype me and dismiss me with a wave of the hand.

It was at school that I was finally allowed the freedom to lose myself in anonymity, to transcend cultural typecasting. In my jeans, running around campus on my way to class, I was disentangled enough from Little Havana and from the pain in my past to begin to feel somewhat secure and accepted. College provided the comfortable stability that I had missed for so long.

I clearly remember my first snowfall. I had made a pact with Liz, the girl whose room adjoined mine, that she would wake me immediately the moment the first snow started falling. Liz—a tall, lanky New Yorker—was true to her promise. One night in November, a little after midnight, I was awakened by persistent knocks at my door. It was Liz in her nightclothes, her auburn hair tucked tightly under a bright green woolen cap.

"Let's go, amiga," she told me, and we ran outdoors in our boots and flannel pajamas, laughing and slipping on the blue-tinted ice.

Snow! How different it felt and tasted from what I had

imagined—much less like cotton than I expected. How miraculous that it should cover the whole earth as far as the eye could see! Periodically hurling snowballs at each other, we roamed until dawn the quiet streets of the New England town that I now called home.

It was at the college that I began to sort out the anecdotes which make up the bulk of this book. It was a painful process, compiling an account that candidly depicted some of the agony and confusion felt by my people. It was painful on my own account, too. When you leave a place forever, leave all that is dear to you behind—the language, the culture, the trivia of your daily existence—the void is enormous. You feel a range of emotions difficult to articulate, especially in an adopted language.

Although I missed Mami and Papi terribly, I purposefully avoided returning to Miami during vacations. Whenever I went back, I was inevitably reminded of how uncomfortable it feels to be the intruder, the homeless and unwanted refugee. How quickly people forget that they themselves are descendants of immigrants!

I clung to the precarious security that my new surroundings offered me, lapping up every bit of acceptance and understanding that flowed my way. Whenever I did return to Miami, my mastery of English brought with it opportunities to glimpse "the Cuban problem" from a different angle. I could now cross ethnic lines at will. I often mingled among native Americans, pretending to be one of them. Many times I explained my slight and unidentifiable accent by saying that I had lived abroad as a child. People believed me, often sharing openly with me their true feelings about the "spics." I attended many a party in Miami where I was graphically given the horrifyingly stereotyped descriptions of "those people." At times, I was confidentially told that Cubans are loud and dirty and lazy; that they are a nuisance and a drain on Federal funds.

"All of them are on welfare, you know," an attractive medical student once said to me over a daiquiri.

"Tell me more about them," I asked, feigning ignorance.

Sometimes people's descriptions were puzzlingly contradictory. A dentist once shared with me at great length his feelings regarding "these Cubans," while expertly drilling into one of my upper teeth.

"Those people are really industrious. They're like the Jews. They are willing to work for lower wages, so they get most of the jobs," he said knowingly. After that incident, I purposely saved my medical complaints until I returned to the haven of my northern school.

I would often admit to being Cuban after a few particularly stinging remarks.

"You don't look Cuban," most would uncomfortably reply, once more avoiding my eyes. Bigots have a hard time explaining exceptions. People that don't fit their stereotypes tend to make them feel uncomfortable. Sometimes friends of mine, temporarily forgetting my background, breezily made derogatory generalizations in my presence about "the spics." At such moments I was forced to choose between two distasteful alternatives: ignoring thoughtless comments not intended to hurt me personally, or creating a scene.

I had mixed emotions when I actually became a citizen of the United States. It was a hot summer day, and Mami and Papi accompanied me. They were not quite ready to make this kind of commitment themselves, yet they understood that I had grown up with one foot in each culture, feeling strong ties to both Cuba and the United States. It was now time for me to become an American citizen. The procedure itself was rather comical. First, I was led into a room filled to the brim with foreigners. To the casual observer it must have seemed a sort of convention of United Nations representatives. My name and country of origin were called out. I stood. A judge dressed in full regalia asked me to renounce all allegiance to my country of birth. I raised my right hand and firmly stated that I did, crossing my fingers behind my back. I became an American by alphabetical order. People clapped and congratulated me while Mami and Papi silently cried in the back of the room.

The day I formally became an American, a delegation of the Daughters of the American Revolution, wearing impeccable white gloves, gave each of us new citizens a miniature American flag. They shook our hands and wished us luck. I wondered where they had all been when we needed a word of encouragement as disoriented foreigners. Afterwards, a very Irish-looking young lawyer read us our newly acquired rights. His words made a lot of the people in the room sob. We were now one hundred percent American, even if only on paper. We could now vote people into office and were free to speak out even against the President, and not get shot! America. These days I actually forget sometimes that I'm an immigrant. I'm reminded when people inevitably detect an accent and curiously ask me where I'm "originally" from. It's a question I hear at least a time or two on any given day. It gets to be repetitious. Whenever I'm asked, I'm flooded with memories that only another refugee can genuinely understand.

It never ceases to amaze me how universal the refugee experience actually is. Names change, the countries from which immigrants come are different, but the adjusting process remains uncannily the same. Our reasons for coming are almost identical: to seek a better life; to live without repression, without fear; to be and to let be; to better our situation; to offer our children the chance to realize their potential; to be free.

The assimilation process, too, remains similar for all immigrants: the fears, the ponderous alienation, the language barrier, the inevitable rejections, the problems that invariably arise from the head-on collision of differing ways of living and thinking. People diffuse into the melting pot while still trying to preserve whatever they sense is of value from the old ways.

Often, seemingly innocent events trigger off a myriad of inappropriate reactions. For instance, harmless firecrackers hurled during festivities are particularly traumatic for me. They resemble too much the sounds of war, sounds I want to forget but intuitively know I never will.

Human-interest stories concerning Vietnamese children acclimating themselves to America inevitably make me cry. I react impatiently to those tears, as I always feel that I am wallowing in self-pity and crying for myself rather than for them. It is their turn now, I say to myself, knowing exactly what's ahead for them. My feelings of empathy nevertheless make me want to reach out and try to ameliorate their all-too-real pain.

I myself am still not fully acclimated. Sometimes I dream in English, at other times in Spanish. Sometimes Mami, who speaks as little English today as she did ten years ago, discourses fluently with me in English, in my dreams.

I still count in Spanish. Having first learned my numbers in that language, I find that I can still count faster that way.

I love being bilingual. I can enjoy the poetry of Pablo Neruda as well as that of Shelley and Keats. I don't have to resort to translations. Often, a particular word in one language perfectly describes what in the other is, at best, inadequately expressed. I still vacillate, swaying at times unsteadily between my two totally different backgrounds, only now they don't rage within me as they once did. They complement each other better and better every day.

At times I wish I could have experienced a normal American childhood. I would have enjoyed going away to camp. I want to obliterate the painful memories that are such a large part of my past, to have instead a collection of typical, relaxed, happy childhood memories. I yearn to experience that carefree exuberance only a child can know, and I regret that I grew up before my time. But the innocence of childhood, once lost, can never be recaptured.

Sometimes I feel great pride in having made it without the many advantages offered the native American. I know that I am stronger for having been forced to make my own way, for having had to overcome as many obstacles as I did. "Pain builds character," generations of sages have concluded, and I concur. Unfortunately, it also hurts.

I have learned firsthand that the only certainty in life is its very uncertainty. The only thing that you can unconditionally depend on is yourself. I am most independent and self-sufficient these days. Having your very existence turned to shambles by factors not in your control makes you aware of the bittersweet fact that security is only an illusion.

I regret not having been raised in a house with an attic filled with treasured mementos that go back for generations. I've missed not having a sense of continuity with what was left behind. I wish that I could visit Cuba. I want to embrace once more those that I've never seen since I left. I want to walk into the home of my childhood and come to terms, fully and finally, with my past. Memories and regrets are all that remain, not only for me, but for all of us.

I am very ambivalent about diplomatic relations being re-established with Cuba. On the one hand, I look forward to visiting my old country. Yet renewed relations also mean accepting as fact the idea that the new order is here to stay. Maybe I also delude myself at times into thinking that a drastic change could magically come about. Cubans understandably have a hard time being objective about Cuba. I constantly remind myself to be, but know that I can never truly be.

Mami and Papi have made as good an adjustment as they've been able to. They associate primarily with Cubans, maintain a Cuban meal schedule, and subscribe to numerous Spanish publications. They still live vaguely convinced of the fantasy that they will soon return home.

Dad manages a store in Miami these days. Mother is as hooked on soap operas as many other middle-aged American housewives. Whenever I see her, I detect that she is no longer tenaciously fighting the fate that our country's upheaval thrust on her. Her new acceptance of her situation reassures me.

My grandfather finally immigrated to the States. After he left Cuba, it took him several months to realize that he could once again freely discuss conditions on the island. He imagined that numerous government spies were crouched outside behind the foliage, concerned solely with those events taking place inside our house. He compulsively checked and rechecked doors and windows for evidence that those agents were indeed tampering with the house. He lowered his voice and glanced uneasily around the room whenever he spoke of what he had seen and experienced in Cuba. Even now, he is still wonderfully amazed at the American's right to freedom of speech. He still can't believe that we can talk out loud against the policies of those in power without being shot or put in jail. He still has trouble believing that he is free. Grandfather became an American citizen only last year. He cried like a baby.

My mother occasionally gets letters from Tata, who is now playing lady of the house in our home in Cuba.

After Dad left Cuba, the militia arrived at our house so that a formal inventory could be filed. They asked Tata if she had anywhere to go. Tata has no other family and had worked for us for so long that she felt as if the house were her own.

The government allowed her to continue to live there.

"It is your duty to maintain the house as before. It is against the law for you or anyone to take anything out," they said.

The men made a complete inventory. Tata was told that even if a plate broke, she was not allowed to throw it away.

"Keep the pieces for us in a box," she was told. "Whenever we are back for a periodic inspection, you can show us what may have broken during our absence. Enjoy it, and *Viva la Revolución!*"

A few years ago we read in the *Diario Las Americas*, Miami's largest Latin newspaper, that a group of Cubans had been picked up at sea after escaping from the island on a boat named the *Capri*. The article went on to describe Dad's boat in Havana perfectly. We tried to trace the boat in the hope that the authorities would return it to us, the proper owners. We soon gave up. How could we even begin to prove our right of ownership?

I still visit Miami with reluctance. Too painful, too many memories I'd rather forget. I treasure the anonymity that living away from Little Havana affords me. My years in Miami have left a bitter aftertaste.

I met an American man in college. We fell in love and eventually got married. I pay my taxes. Your everyday problems are my problems. Our hopes for the future are the same. I am an integral part of the American middle class. I play tennis and read *Newsweek*. I have bought, on credit, the American dream. I serve my family an occasional hamburger. The battle of the hemline has caught my imagination as well.

Last year I stopped in Miami for two days on my way down to the Caribbean. It had been several years since my last visit, and I was eager to see old friends. The airport seemed less intimidating than it used to. I guess that just being able to read the signs was helpful and reassuring. Yet too little had changed. The Americans still avoided my eyes on the street. Being able to speak flawless English does not really open all the doors. I got into an argument over dinner with an old friend of my husband's and his wife. They are both Americans and are now living in Miami.

"Why can't your people learn English? Why can't they be assimilated more quickly into the mainstream of American society?" he asked.

"How many days do you have to spare, so that I may tell you a little bit about us?" I replied.

One afternoon, I encountered a classmate of mine from the Mother of Jesus School outside an apartment building on 8th Street. Instantly recognizing each other, we ran toward each other with outstretched arms. We hadn't seen each other in years, and we embraced with shouts of joy. Ironically, we had both lived for years in Miami unaware of our nearly identical predicament.

We greeted each other in Spanish, momentarily unconcerned with that very American axiom that demands a minimum of public emotionality. We were quickly and forcefully brought to our senses and reminded that we were no longer in our own country. Suddenly, we were soaked, drenched in hot water which mercilessly poured from one of the windows of the building.

"Shut up and go back to where you came from," shouted an elderly woman in a harsh and nasal voice.

Looking up, we could see a mass of curlers bobbing up and down from within the building. We never saw the woman's face.

Holding hands, we ran from the scalding water that still poured down from the woman's window. We actually laughed together about the incident while drying ourselves at my friend's house. Not that we were not hurt by what had just happened to us; prejudice, if too frequently experienced, tends to blot out or numb the accompanying pain. By then, we were both immune to the hurt. Subtle forms of prejudice are more insidious, more difficult to identify and deal with. This stranger's hatred was so direct that all we could do was shrug our shoulders and go on.

I also went to visit Aunt Ramona, who teased me about being so thin that I now resembled an Anglo. We solemnly lit a candle in honor of the Virgin Mary.

"So that we may soon go home," she said. I did not have the heart to share my reservations with her. She asked me about my experiences up north. Was it true that it was a little easier for us up there? I candidly replied that it was, as she shook her head in disbelief.

I drove by the Marlin Guest House. It seemed smaller and seedier than I had remembered it. I stopped at the Virgin of the Caridad Cafe on 6th Street. It is a little restaurant decorated with colorful tropical murals done in oils. Plastic flowers rest in the center of all of the tables. The tables themselves are covered with checkered, plastic tablecloths. A young, round waiter jovially asked me in Spanish if I was ready to order. He knew instantly that I was one of them. I ordered an espresso. He smiled. His hair, slicked back and as black as my espresso, contrasted beautifully with his sugar-white teeth.

After serving me, he joined a little freckled-faced blonde patiently waiting for him by the cash register. Speaking excitedly in English to each other, they made arrangements to meet after he finished his shift. Something about a party at Enrique's, he said. Maybe things were changing after all.

149

I wondered about the many tales that I was certain he could share with me. I suddenly realized that the two of us were but a small part of something begun hundreds of years ago. Many had come to these shores before us; many more were bound to follow. The names and nationalities would differ, but their reasons for coming would remain painfully unchanged.

My bill came to thirty-two cents. I left him a dollar tip and walked outside onto the sunlit Miami street. I have not returned since.

Epilogue

I LEARNED SEVERAL MONTHS after completing *A Cuban Story* that the restriction on refugees traveling back to Cuba had suddenly been lifted. Papi immediately began negotiations for a visa for us to return there for a visit. We acted quickly, as we had learned from past experience that, as far as Cuba was concerned, circumstances could be changed rapidly without prior notification. We were eager to return and did not want to miss the opportunity to see members of our family and our country of birth once again, perhaps for the last time.

After several months of supplying the Cuban authorities with vast amounts of background information and individual certificates of good conduct from our local police, Papi, my husband, and I boarded a chartered Belize Airways flight to Havana. An eight-day tourist visa had finally been granted each of us. Our American passports were not recognized by the Cuban authorities, and we had been issued new Cuban ones, which Papi kept glancing at in disbelief. Mami had declined to accompany us. She could not face seeing the Cuba of today, and we had not pressed her to come along.

As the plane approached the Jose Marti Airport, we could see symmetrical, green, rolling hills dotted by numerous palm trees. We were anxious, excited, and fearful. Uncertainty had colored our trip from its earliest stages of planning. We had not even been told when or on what airline we would be flying until that very morning. We felt unprotected without American backing, yet compelled to return.

Papi, who never takes sedatives, was somewhat sleepy from the medication he'd been given by Mami at take-off. He was also frightened. He had heard stories of returning refugees being imprisoned or charged a high tax contingent on the circumstances of their escape. He was terrified to land, fearful of the reception that awaited us, yet he wanted to see his country again before he died.

The plane, filled except for my husband with Cuban refugees, many returning for the first time in twenty years, was strangely silent. Several of the passengers began to cry as we approached the runway.

Initially what struck all of us was how few cars could be seen on the roads during our approach. The formerly bustling area immediately surrounding the airport was strangely deserted. We could see from the window of the plane a few vintage American cars parked along the Rancho Boyeros Road leading to the airport.

It was hot inside the terminal, and we waited nervously to get through the endless procedures required to complete our entry. We had each been allowed forty-four pounds of luggage, yet little of it was actually for personal use.

Mami had sent along clothing and toiletries for Aunt Alicia and other family members. She had painstakingly sewed additional zippers onto the clothing, as we knew how difficult it was for people to obtain them in Cuba. We were anxious about the possibility of having our gifts confiscated. As a precaution, I had scratched up the soles of the new shoes we were bringing in. We wanted the authorities to think that the several pairs of shoes we carried with us were for personal use; yet how could I explain the size sixteen dresses in my suitcase or the five bottles of shampoo and six tubes of toothpaste? Happily, we made it through customs with no problem. That ordeal completed, we boarded a Soviet-made tour bus and slowly wound our way to the Havana Hilton Hotel, now called the Havana Libre, or "Free Havana."

Upon our arrival at what was to be our home for the next week, we were briefed as a group and instructed to carry our identification papers with us at all times. We could visit Aunt Alicia at her home, but she would not be allowed to enter the premises of our room. We had to show our papers at the door whenever we returned to the hotel and again when we entered the elevator. At the hotel restaurant, we had to show our identification papers at the door. In exchange, we were issued a card which we handed to the headwaiter. Our waiter then issued us a meal ticket which allowed us to approach the buffet table. At that point we submitted the card and were finally served. It was irrelevant that we eventually got to know the waiters and elevator operators by name. We still had to show the papers. There were so many bits of paper to keep track of that we would remain somewhat confused throughout the week as to what exactly to show whom.

We joked about the irony that a hotel described as "free" imposed so many limitations on its guests.

How vastly different the city seemed! Havana appeared to be a city in ruins. Very little new building has taken place, and the old structures have sat for years simply crumbling and decaying in the sun. The moist Caribbean air has accelerated the deterioration process in buildings previously immersed in historic quaintness. Whole sections occasionally fall away from the buildings onto the ground. Paint is so scarce that the once shining city has taken on a slumlike appearance, which saddened us immensely.

Residents now use a complex system of wooden timbers, both columns and beams, on the outside and inside of buildings to support the wall structure. Occasionally whole balconies are supported in this haphazard fashion. At times, horizontal beams are placed between two buildings collapsing toward each other, just to hold them precariously up.

We roamed the city, plagued with a sinking feeling of disappointment. Aunt Alicia's former home is presently a foreign embassy, so we wistfully drove by it, unable to enter, and continued the trip in our hired cab to where she now lives. We climbed up the stairs to her humble new apartment, and there she was, the now-fragile little woman whom I so clearly remembered. Seeing and holding her after a sixteen-year separation brought us all to tears. She was like a small child at Christmas, rummaging with glee through the suitcase filled with presents we had brought her. Her hair now has a bluish tint to it because in desperation she has tried to dye it with a lotion designed to cure skin infections. Alicia had never seen a pair of panty hose and inspected them with awe, thinking they were a scarf.

The contrast was immense between her building's shabby exterior and the meticulously clean interior, which was furnished with several beautiful relics from the past. I marveled at the juxtaposition of hand-cut crystal and a leaking bucket used to flush the toilet manually.

For days the matriarchal Alicia had been preparing a welcoming feast in our honor. She had spent a large sum of money obtaining provisions through the black market, where a chicken now costs over 20 pesos. The government allots you one chicken breast a week.

Doctor Antonia, a rotund older woman and close family friend, had prepared delicious *croquetas* and succulent fried plantains. The display of hospitality was touching, almost excessive. We forced ourselves to eat sparingly because we did not want to use up their precious food.

"Almost like the old days, Manuel?" asked Alicia, lovingly holding Papi's hand.

People from our past flocked to the apartment to hear tales about America from the gusanos. We learned that we were no longer called gusanos but *comunitarios* (people from the community). We learned that Dorticos is no longer called "president" and that he has been relegated to a minor position at the Ministry.

We were told how careful we must be about expressing our impressions openly.

"Trust nobody," my aunt said.

Antonia told us how her husband had been jailed the year before for buying black market meat and discussing its purchase with a "friend."

"Only God knows when he'll be released, if ever," Antonia said, shaking her head.

Cousin Francisco had been sent on military service to Ethiopia. He had not been heard from in months. Our tight family group was forever dispersed. We spent a day looking through old photograph albums, trying to recapture glimpses of a life seemingly lived a thousand years ago. Laughing and crying intermittently, we became immersed in the past. Dusk found us drinking the coffee we'd managed to get through customs with us and still talking animatedly.

". . . and what happened to Jose . . . and to Carmen?" Endlessly went the questions. Some are now in America, others in Puerto Rico, New York, Spain–others are dead . . . or in jail. We briefly contemplated recovering the valuables concealed by Papi prior to his departure. Alicia's reaction of horror at the mere suggestion of this confirmed unequivocally for us the lunacy of the idea. We couldn't even begin to formulate a viable plan of recovery, much less carry it out, within a period of less than eight days. We would have had to work at night with the help of a trusted friend proficient in the use of tools. The risks involved were tremendous. Had we been able to salvage anything of value, the problem of actually transporting it out of the country remained insurmountable. We opted not to attempt to recover anything.

We were shown with great secrecy the latest ration books. We laid one of them on the floor and took a picture of it.

- —4 packs of cigarettes a month
- —1 pair of shoes a year
- —1 bar of soap a month
- —1 roll of toilet paper every six months
- —4 meters of material a year or two ready-made dresses
- —3 cans of condensed milk every thirty-four days
- —½ pound of cooking oil a month
- —2 packs of matches a month
- —Every other Saturday coffee is available. Four ounces may be bought to last fifteen days.
- —2 pounds of potatoes every other month
- —meat once a month

The itemized list went on and on.

Aunt Alicia had not been able to purchase sheets for the beds in ten years or seen toothpaste, talcum powder, or deodorant for more than a year.

Antonia had been forced to spend one year of medical duty in the countryside away from her children, and could no longer work in private practice.

"I punch a time clock now. If I arrive late a couple of days in any given month, my case is brought before a medical committee consisting of my colleagues and I'm reprimanded."

I was amazed by the inconsistencies within the system. In some professions salaries are fixed, and no incentives exist to perform a job well. Workers do not even fear being fired. Just the day before, we had heard of a bus driver who left the passengers on his bus stranded at a curb while he caught a ride home for lunch. Only hours later did he bother to come back and drive the still-waiting people to their destination.

It was boiling hot inside the apartment and the fan did not work, so I suggested that we all walk over to a nearby beach for a swim. Everyone laughed.

"That beach is now a military club open only to army personnel. We are each assigned a beach we can swim in. The one we are assigned to is so far away that it's not worth bothering to go so late in the afternoon."

Hearing an unusual squeal coming from above the apartment, I inquired about it.

"The neighborhood is fattening up some pigs on the roof with leftovers. We kill the animals at night and divide the meat among those who have contributed their scraps."

Going into the bedroom a little later, I impulsively turned on Alicia's ancient television set and was irritated to find a Russian film without Spanish subtitles. For a few minutes I tried to follow the plot, concentrating on the meaningless chatter uttered by the actors. Finally, in frustration, I turned the black-and-white set off.

"You should buy a new TV," I said without thinking as I strolled back into the living room. A heavy sigh was heard throughout the room. I immediately understood the absurdity of my remark. Why bother to watch programs that you can't understand or programs that are so fraught with propaganda as to make them neither worthwhile nor enjoyable?

Alicia began to explain the problem to me.

"Only esteemed workers are eligible to have their names

added to the request list for such luxury items as televisions. First you must prove your loyalty by participating in a minimum of sixty-three 'volunteer' activities a year. Additionally, you must regularly donate blood and attend the weekly study groups in your neighborhood, where photocopies of Fidelito's speeches are studied and discussed at length. Then, maybe, you get your name on the list. It's just not worth the bother. Who wants to pick potatoes for forty-five days with no guarantees of compensation?"

Tina, my aunt's neighbor, began to comment on the high suicide rate among the young.

"It's as if they know intuitively that there is something better, a more desirable way to live. For many of us the despair we feel is just too overwhelmingly painful. We live without hope, without dreams."

Antonia interjected that a colleague had spent months on a research project trying to find a pool of a hundred volunteers who had not taken any sedatives whatsoever within the past six months. He desisted after realizing that it was an impossible task. "Every day I'm myself flooded with an overwhelming number of requests for 'nerve pills'; the severity of the problem worries me greatly."

We could bear to hear no more. We asked Alicia and Tina to have lunch on the following day at our hotel, as a special permit could be obtained at the desk. They gratefully accepted our invitation, and we bid our farewells.

The following day we had Tico, a friend of Alicia's, pick us up at the hotel. Cabs are so scarce that independent cabbies—drivers without the government's sanction—work covertly on the side. Tico, an eighty-year-old, jolly little man, came for us at 9 A.M. in his 1952 Ford. The day before, our cabbie had been complaining about how many restrictions the government imposed on him and had cursed the Transportation Minister for his total ignorance of the transportation industry.

"You just can't put a guy with no experience in the field into a powerful job like that simply because his loyalty to the state stands unquestioned," he had said with a frustrated look on his face.

My husband wanted to find out from Tico how the gasoline situation was in Cuba.

"What you get a month depends on what kind of car you have. I get eight gallons a month for good old Berta here," he said, patting the dashboard. "You can get up to twenty gallons a month," he continued. "I get the rest that I need in the black market, at $1.80 a gallon."

We drove down the Quinta Avenida towards Marianao, passing the Vedado area, whose stench we could smell from inside the car.

Tico noticed my grimace and explained.

"Garbage is collected every fifteen days."

Waiting for a traffic light to change, we were accosted by a poorly dressed old beggar who thrust his bent, arthritic hand toward my face. Papi hurled him some change and, thanking us profusely, he walked on.

It was evident by now that people recognized us on the streets as being either comunitarios or foreign tourists. The poorly dressed crowds constantly followed us at a distance, and children approached us asking for gum.

Clearly remembering the route toward our house, I instructed Tico on which street to take. We traveled northward, toward the ocean. I could feel my palms sweating and could almost hear the accelerating beats inside my chest as we approached my street. Suddenly I saw the home of my childhood looming in the distance.

How can I convey the emotion that overtook me as I

approached my house? Jumping out of the car, I ran toward the front door with Papi following close behind.

Every window had been broken or removed long ago. Wooden slats replaced the glass panels in places. In sections of the house, large wooden panels covered entire windows. They hung precariously, tacked on by nails. The exterior of the house was in shambles and the grass on the lawn reached my shoulders. I sensed people observing me intently from behind the upstairs wooden slats.

It was a nightmare, a bad dream I knew I'd never awake from. I began to cry. Large heaving sobs shook my body. Involuntary spasms took hold of me. My reaction was so visceral, it frightened me. I longed to faint and take refuge in unconsciousness.

I began to yell for Tata, who I'd heard still lived there. "Tata, Tata, it's Marcia Fuentes. I'm home."

A familiar voice answered, and I could hear the sounds of heavy steps running down the staircase. The door burst open and I was engulfed in a strong and reassuringly familiar embrace.

"I'm home, I'm home!" I kept repeating as though to convince myself that it was true.

Tata's cheeks were bathed in tears. Her gray hair was pulled back from her face. Her gentle hands, spotted brown by age and the Caribbean sun, touched my face between them. We held each other in silence, finding solace in the warmth of each other's body.

A hundred questions came to mind. How was she? Who else lived now in my home? Why had the once-beautiful house been allowed to rot away as if struck by the destructive force of a hurricane?

We learned that some months after Papi's departure the militia had methodically emptied the house. The downstairs had been temporarily converted into a school. We could see the tattered remains of a desk in what had once been my room. The rest of the downstairs remained disconcertingly empty, littered with rotting mango skins and rusting cans. A family now lived in what had been the garage.

Tata took us upstairs, where three separate families now lived. The left upstairs bedroom which faced the ocean was now Tata's. We could hear the ocean waves breaking against the rocks but were not able to see out the windows, as they were boarded up.

A familiar landscape painting caught my eye, hanging incongruously above the portable burner Tata now used for cooking. A broken night table brought back a memory or two. All that remained was shattered bits of the past, memories and regrets.

We could hear the cry of a child coming from the next room. Approaching the sobbing sounds, I entered what had been a small study. I had always associated it with the smell of leather and cigars.

A dilapidated brown crib now sat in the middle of the room. A golden-haired little girl, no older than two years, stood there crying and chewing distractedly on the hem of her blue-and-white checkered cotton dress. I saw my old doll Carmela propped against the crib's back corner. Her head rested on its side, severed from the rest of the body. She was naked and streaks of caked mud covered her front. I instinctively approached her, trying to put back together her broken body, to no avail. The child continued to cry.

Tata and my husband quietly entered the room behind me. I could feel their eyes piercing my back.

"Marcia, Carmela is little Maria's favorite doll. Remember how she was your favorite too?" said Tata, intuitively trying to appease me.

My husband was able to reattach Carmela's head, and the child stopped crying.

I wanted to leave this house whose present condition left me feeling so empty. For a second I wished that I had never returned but had maintained intact the image of my home, the cornerstone inside my mind where most of the lovely images from my past solidly rested.

Clumsily maneuvering over the filth that now engulfed the yard, I walked outside expecting to see my dollhouse. The yard was strangely empty, as if the little house had never existed, as if it had just been a figment of my feverish imagination.

"They actually had a family living there for a while! The salt air rotted it to a point that it had to be demolished. It was just breeding too many rats," said Tata.

There was nothing else to see. Reluctantly, I said good-bye to Tata, whose dear face I knew I'd never see again, and hurriedly walked back to Tico, patiently waiting by the car.

We drove on down the Quinta Avenida, sporadically jolted by the numerous potholes dotting the road, and approached the old Mother of Jesus School. A high barbed wire fence and an aging guard barred our way. We explained my longing to see my school and maybe photograph it. The guard refused vehemently. We were told that it was now the College of Medicine and that neither visitors nor photographs were allowed.

The absurdity of what he was saying made me cry harder. No rational explanations were given, just inflexible mandates from above. I hated the man's smug, lined face, the insolent tilt of his hat. *He* was the intruder, not I, and I wanted to wipe off his contemptuous smirk.

Realizing the futility of our request, we turned around and left. Thanks to Antonia, I was able later in the week to visit the school under the guise of being her assistant. As she had several personal contacts in the medical community, she was able to obtain for us a false pass.

That visit too was depressing. The once-spotless marble floors were now littered with beer bottles and cigarette butts. All religious paintings had been removed, and in their place hung large color photographs of Fidelito and Che Guevara. The chapel had been dismantled, and assorted hearts and livers inside formaldehyde jars rested on what had formerly been the altar.

I was angered by the smells and the desecration I witnessed. How efficiently they had obliterated every vestige from the past! I could hear no sounds coming from the classrooms. We left the building and drove in silence to the cemetery where my grandmother lay buried.

Bewildered, we entered the administrative office and pored through the records, which were catalogued by date of death. We then walked slowly about the mausoleums, recognizing a familiar name here and there until at last we found the shady spot where Grandma now rested. Cleaning the site of litter, I placed some white gardenias on the grave and took a photograph for Mami, with Papi smiling self-consciously for the camera.

That night we drove aimlessly about the unlit city, sporadically stopping to read the overwhelming number of lengthy political billboards which have replaced all advertising. We listened to the constant propaganda on the radio, amazed at the vicious content of the programming. Stopping at the Malecon, we sat and listened to the ocean waves crashing against the rocks. A small, thin boy, no older than seven, approached us and asked if we were Russians. When we told him we lived in America, he shouted, "The American exploit the Cubans. The Cubans exploit the Americans. They all hate each other and I'm really confused." A sullen woman in her thirties quickly took hold of his arm and whisked him away.

Since in Cuba there are separate shops where only foreigners can buy, we spent an afternoon at Intur, formerly Sears, near the Prado area.

Intur has no windows in order to minimize the understandable discontent the locals feel at the discrepancy in the selection that is offered them and the tourists. Again we had to show our passports to an armed, youthful militiaman stationed at the door. I noted that this made it the forty-eighth time we had been forced to show some kind of identification during our stay.

The interior was austere and utilitarian—no frills, no props or guile to entice the shopper to spend more. We were shocked at the high prices and at the proliferation of American products for sale. We saw a pair of Lee jeans selling for the equivalent of $124, a bottle of cognac for $144, one roll of Polaroid film for $48, a can of Campbell's chicken noodle soup for $2.76, and a miniscule refrigerator for $2,415. Needless to say, we opted for leaving my family all our remaining cash to be spent on the black market, rather than buying for them at Intur the goods that they desperately needed.

One day, terribly curious as to who was now living in Grandma's house, we ventured into her building on Amistad Street, which was located not far from our hotel. Climbing up the creaking stairs, I was despondent at finding the once meticulously kept building in a dreadful state of disrepair. Much to our surprise, Carlos, Aunt Sonia's widower, was still living there. When he answered our knocks, Carlos did not immediately recognize us and Papi kept laughing and saying to him, "Okay, idiot, tell me who I am . . . come on, dumbbell, who does this face belong to?"

Recognition finally surfaced on Carlos's brown face. It lit up like a star as Carlos and Papi hugged and kissed. Overtaken by emotion, I could only look on.

"Manuel, my God, I can't believe it's you!"

164

Carlos glanced uneasily behind us and ceremoniously showed us inside. The once almost cluttered apartment was now furnished with two discolored beach chairs and an old cot. A few tattered shirts hung suspended on a makeshift clothesline strung across the living room. I saw the partial remains of the flowery pink wallpaper whose designs I used to love to trace and later color with crayons whenever I visited Grandma.

"Pretty pathetic, don't you agree? I'd put on a shirt for you, but these days I use them only to leave the house," said Carlos with a wave of his hand.

To my dismay, Carlos insisted on showing us the rest of the apartment. I did not wish to see any more. I did not want to confront visually the skeletal remains of Grandma's little place. Overwhelmed by the discrepancies between past and present, I felt agonizingly bewildered by the sights and smells brutally thrust upon me by my country's stark new way of life.

You could no longer walk down the hallway, as the whole corridor was supported by the timbers we'd been encountering so often throughout Havana.

"It's just not worth it to keep up furniture. Just to paint a chair I've got to get three separate permits, and then I've got to carry the damn chair downtown on my back. There's no paint anyway . . . boy, I could have used your help last week! I had to bring my cot back from being repaired. *My* cot. Funny, it's not *my* cot anymore, it's everyone's—I just slip back sometimes into my old way of talking."

Just then there was a knock at the door, and Carlos simply looked at us with his brown, frightened eyes. Cautiously, he approached the door and heaved a sigh of relief when he encountered a trusted neighbor.

"You can't ever be sure. Last week the Committee for the Defense of the Revolution member assigned to my block came to check on what he'd earlier seen me bring into the house in a paper bag," said Carlos, wiping his forehead with his hands.

He began to tell us all about the twenty-one homes Fidelito maintains throughout the island. It is said that he never sleeps two nights in a row in the same one. We heard about Cuba's being divided into fourteen rather than six provinces, and about Christmas now being celebrated on July 26, a revolutionary holiday.

Carlos proudly told us how he'd been elected to the thirteen-member Special Review Board for his neighborhood.

"I'm to investigate potential gusanos. The position gives me a chance to help a lot of people, given that I'm a gusano myself," he said with a grin. "It also minimizes the chances of my being sent to jail. Although there is no space anyway, even for common criminals. What I need is a vacation."

We asked him to join us at Varadero for the weekend. Carlos laughed.

"Hotels are prioritized. First come the tourists, then local honeymooners. It would cost me 500 pesos for a week in Varadero, if and when I could obtain a permit."

I mentioned that I wanted to go to Bibijagua on the Isle of Pines, now the Isle of Youth. I collect unusual sands from all parts of the world and thought that Bibijagua's black marble sand would be a nice addition to my collection.

"Don't bother. The government decided that Bibijagua's sand is too black, so they added some white sand to it."

Carlos then wistfully asked us if in America one could still get part-time jobs on the side to make a little extra money. At that very moment we had a power blackout. Carlos commented calmly that it was a frequent occurrence and continued talking. He told us the story of an official who had returned to the island from a buying spree on behalf of the government. He had mistakenly bought a large order of snowplows, thinking they were used to clean the roads. He was currently in jail. We continued to sit there in the darkness exchanging news and impressions until late into the night.

It was arranged that we'd meet Carlos outside the Havana Libre at 9 P.M. on Friday night. We still had with us an assortment of products that would be invaluable to him. We'd worry about getting the stuff out of the hotel later. With a hopeful look on his face, Carlos wondered if Papi could spare a few pairs of undershorts.

We spent the next day in the country, relieved at not encountering any vast changes. On the white road to Varadero we marveled at the richness of the soil and the lushness of the countryside. We stopped in Santa Marta, where Papi was born. The horse-drawn buggies still traveled about the town as if it were encapsulated in a time warp, or time itself had stopped forty years ago.

Driving through the main square, we stopped to photograph the home Papi had been born in. It is now a restaurant, and we could see through the windows the rows of canned goods lining the back wall. A quick swim in Varadero followed. The miles of white sand and crystal-clear waters remained reassuringly unchanged. Nature had been spared from the decay and destruction all around us, yet how I despised the feeling of being a tourist in my own country! Upon our return to the city, we treated ourselves to dinner at Tropicana below a sky lit up by a thousand stars. To Papi, even the dancing girls seemed less beautiful than he'd remembered. We could see a large vertical cesarean scar on the belly of one of the dancers, and we were sitting so close to the stage that beads of sweat kept flying by our heads.

Wherever we went, we encountered dissatisfied young people who only wanted us to tell them about disco and the latest American films.

In Santa Maria, we met a young man who begged us to deliver for him through customs his parents' wedding pictures. His parents had been living in Miami for quite some time, but he had been unable to join them, as his age made him eligible for military service. He was thus not allowed to leave the country. We agreed to help him get the pictures out and met him at a predetermined time outside the hotel.

Carlos also came over that night, and I pretended to leave the hotel with a personal package so that I could meet him on a street corner near Coppelia and hand over the loot—primarily soap bars, Band-Aids, and Papi's old underwear. He was so grateful that his eyes momentarily watered, and looking furtively around, he hugged me tightly and disappeared forever into the darkness.

The time to leave Cuba once again was upon us. The roommate that Papi had been randomly assigned upon arriving at the hotel finally made his appearance. He had been staying with family in Santiago. A heavyset, middle-aged man wearing a multicolored *guayabera*, Tomas now lived in Puerto Rico. He was accompanied by his emaciated younger brother, who had just been released from jail. The brother didn't say much, just followed Tomas quietly about with an empty stare that said he'd seen too much, or nothing at all, for years.

At 2 P.M. on Sunday, eight days after our arrival, we traveled the Rancho Boyeros Road toward the airport for the last time. Upon arriving, we all waited impatiently for the truck that was following the tour bus with our suitcases. Our bags were finally hurled to us from the truck. They were now so nearly empty that they could be passed above our heads from hands to outstretched hands.

Inside my cigarette case, I had hidden a gold and ruby ring that Aunt Alicia had held in safekeeping for me all these years. I began to worry as I saw the people in line before me

168

having their cigarette packs searched by the militia. I took the case out of my pocket and placed it casually inside my purse. Fortunately, when my turn came, the person assigned to search me placed the purse with all its contents inside the ominous looking X-ray unit on the counter. I held my breath for a few seconds waiting for the concealed ring to give me away, for the unit to begin to buzz loudly. Nothing happened. We were then whisked off to the waiting room, called by Cubans the "fishbowl," from which eight hours later we boarded our plane back to freedom.

From the window of the plane I could see the lights of Havana dimming. I felt strangely detached. I no longer sensed a strong connection binding me to the grand earth below. My country of birth no longer held me captive by an invisible umbilical cord. I was finally purged from the uncertainties of being uprooted and homeless.

I felt a strong kinship with America that I'd never before experienced. Immediately prior to our trip, I'd been struck by the irrational notion that maybe I did belong in Cuba, that my destiny dictated a solid commitment to help improve conditions in my native country. The time had arrived to confront the core of my allegiance. I wanted to evaluate objectively through the eyes of an adult what life was like under this vastly different system. That the initial decision for us to emigrate had been made by my parents, without my consent, weighed heavily on me. Innumerable times I'd faced the possibility that maybe my views on Cuba were colored by a familial bias. Without seeing for myself, I could not fully reject the possibility that my childhood perceptions were basically unfair and erroneous.

Yet this trip had confirmed without a doubt that my parents' choice to leave the island was the correct one. The same choice was now being made by me, this time independently of my family's influence. I saw the alternatives as lucidly as I'd ever seen them. Suddenly it seemed so basic and simple! I remembered the words printed on the first page of my little blue booklet delineating my rights as an American citizen: "You may think as you please. You may speak or write as you please." My eyes watered at the realization that those corny little words said it all for me, and for every single person on that plane.

I looked at Papi, and his peaceful smile told me that he felt as I did. We were in silent agreement as to where our home now was. As the plane landed, a cry of gladness formed in my throat and I shouted, "Hurray for Freedom!" My refugee companions began to clap in unison.

After all the pain and sorrow—after the nightmares, the tears, and the disillusionment—we landed in America. We were finally and unequivocally home.